SPORTS JUMBLE®

WORD POWER WORKOUTS

by Henri Arnold,
Bob Lee,
and Mike Argirion

TRIUMPH
BOOKS
CHICAGO

This book is available at special discounts
for your group or organization.

For further information, contact:

Triumph Books LLC
814 North Franklin Street
Chicago, IL 60610
(800) 888-4741
(312) 337-1807 FAX

ISBN 1-57243-113-X

Printed in the USA

CONTENTS

CLASSIC

DAILY

CHALLENGER

ANSWERS

CLASSIC

SPORTS
JUMBLE®

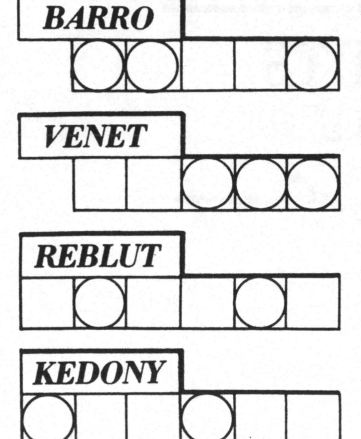

JUMBLE®

Unscramble these four Jumbles,
one letter to each square, to
form four ordinary words.

BARRO

VENET

REBLUT

KEDONY

'py n' year

CHAMP

NOT IF YOU'RE DRIVING TONIGHT

THE LAST GUY TO BOX THIS FIGHTER.

Now arrange the circled letters
to form the surprise answer, as
suggested by the above cartoon.

Print the SURPRISE ANSWER here   THE ⬡⬡⬡⬡⬡⬡⬡⬡⬡⬡⬡

JUMBLE®

Unscramble these four Jumbles, one letter to each square, to form four ordinary words.

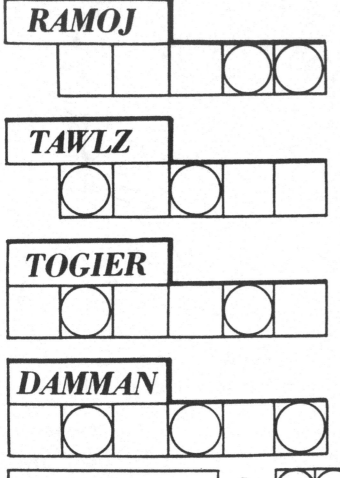

RAMOJ

TAWLZ

TOGIER

DAMMAN

Now I can join that foursome!

WHAT THE COW WHO ATE UP ALL THE GRASS WAS.

Now arrange the circled letters to form the surprise answer, as suggested by the above cartoon.

Print the SURPRISE ANSWER here

A

JUMBLE®

Unscramble these four Jumbles,
one letter to each square, to
form four ordinary words.

FLECT

SOKYM

TOOLEC

BIRDHY

WHAT THE BALLPLAYER
DID AFTER A
LATE NIGHT OUT.

Now arrange the circled letters
to form the surprise answer, as
suggested by the above cartoon.

Print the SURPRISE ANSWER here

" ◯◯◯◯◯ ◯◯◯◯ "

JUMBLE®

Unscramble these four Jumbles, one letter to each square, to form four ordinary words.

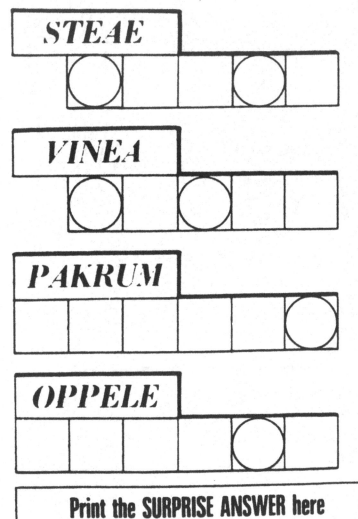

STEAE

VINEA

PAKRUM

OPPELE

Print the SURPRISE ANSWER here

Your horse won!!!

IN | PLACE | SHOW

YOU KNOW YOU
GOT A BREAK WHEN
YOU HAVE THIS!

Now arrange the circled letters to form the surprise answer, as suggested by the above cartoon.

A

JUMBLE®

Unscramble these four Jumbles, one letter to each square, to form four ordinary words.

BYRDE

HOTUM

DINDAC

SORRAY

They'll never make the big time

AFTER A DIRTY GAME, THESE BALLPLAYERS WERE ALL WASHED UP.

Now arrange the circled letters to form the surprise answer, as suggested by the above cartoon.

Print the SURPRISE ANSWER here

THE

JUMBLE®

Unscramble these four Jumbles,
one letter to each square, to
form four ordinary words.

TURTE

PROUG

NEETIC

STELEN

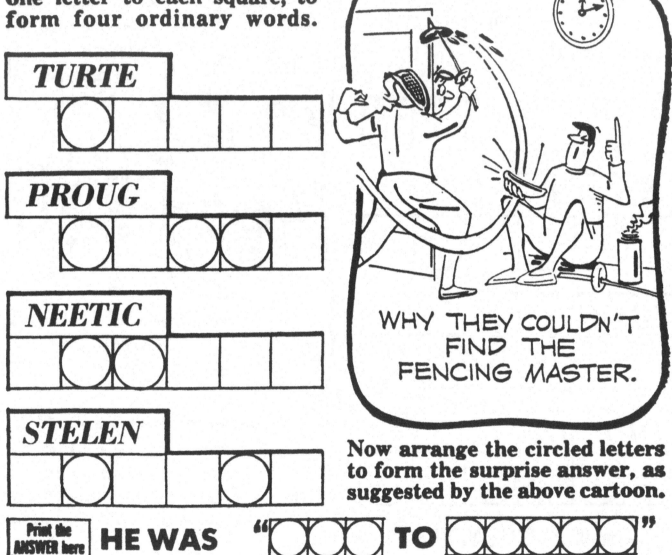

WHY THEY COULDN'T
FIND THE
FENCING MASTER.

Now arrange the circled letters
to form the surprise answer, as
suggested by the above cartoon.

Print the
ANSWER here   HE WAS "◯◯◯ TO ◯◯◯◯◯◯"

JUMBLE®

Unscramble these four Jumbles, one letter to each square, to form four ordinary words.

TELIE

NOMUT

GLOONB

DIOING

Print the SURPRISE ANSWER here

Some pitcher— thinks he's the whole team!

NO BASEBALL TEAM WOULD BE COMPLETE WITHOUT THIS!

Now arrange the circled letters to form the surprise answer, as suggested by the above cartoon.

JUMBLE®

Unscramble these four Jumbles, one letter to each square, to form four ordinary words.

LUDGI

TOSOP

NAITAT

PAMEND

Print the SURPRISE ANSWER here

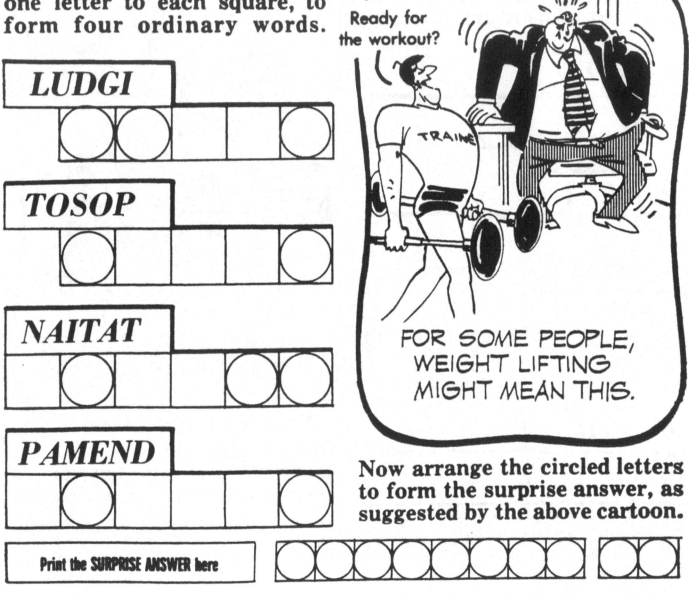

(Puff)

Ready for the workout?

TRAINE

FOR SOME PEOPLE, WEIGHT LIFTING MIGHT MEAN THIS.

Now arrange the circled letters to form the surprise answer, as suggested by the above cartoon.

JUMBLE®

Unscramble these four Jumbles, one letter to each square, to form four ordinary words.

SOPIE

ORRGI

REMMAH

ENGOUT

When do the trained horses come on?

WHAT THE BOXING CHAMP TURNED CIRCUS PERFORMER BECAME.

Now arrange the circled letters to form the surprise answer, as suggested by the above cartoon.

Print the SURPRISE ANSWER here

JUMBLE®

Unscramble these four Jumbles, one letter to each square, to form four ordinary words.

EDDIC

GUGOE

CAVELE

PROPHE

EACH WITH A PAIN.

Now arrange the circled letters to form the surprise answer, as suggested by the above cartoon.

Print the SURPRISE ANSWER here

11

JUMBLE®

Unscramble these four Jumbles,
one letter to each square, to
form four ordinary words.

NEPOR

TAXEC

YIHRTT

LAYGEL

Escaped!

ANIMALS YOU MIGHT
FIND ON THE
GOLF COURSE.

Now arrange the circled letters
to form the surprise answer, as
suggested by the above cartoon.

Print the SURPRISE ANSWER here

12

JUMBLE®

Unscramble these four Jumbles,
one letter to each square, to
form four ordinary words.

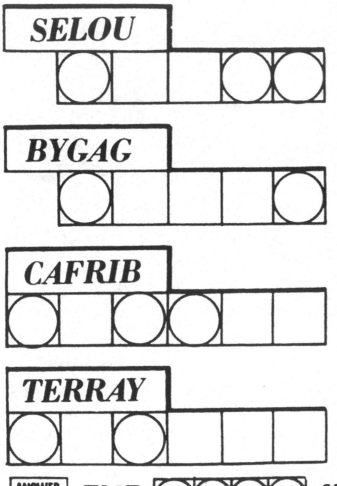

SELOU

BYGAG

CAFRIB

TERRAY

WHAT THE BALL-
PLAYERS WANTED
FROM CITY HALL.

Now arrange the circled letters
to form the surprise answer, as
suggested by the above cartoon.

  THE ☐☐☐☐ IN THE

JUMBLE®

Unscramble these four Jumbles,
one letter to each square, to
form four ordinary words.

GUCOH

TURSY

TALLEB

RUFTUE

WHAT THE CRAZY
ROWER WHO FELL
OUT OF HIS RACING
BOAT WAS.

Now arrange the circled letters
to form the surprise answer, as
suggested by the above cartoon.

Print the SURPRISE ANSWER here

OF HIS

14

JUMBLE®

Unscramble these four Jumbles, one letter to each square, to form four ordinary words.

YOWLL

REGUP

ROTTAH

ABBIDE

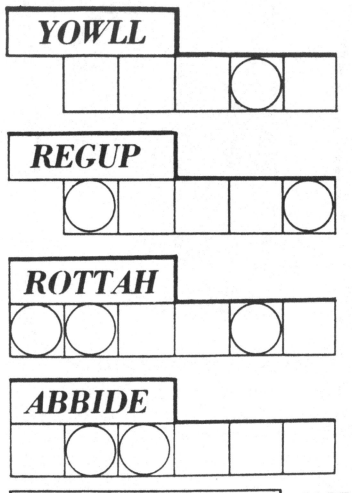

Two bucks on my kid

A GOOD BET FOR FIRST GRADERS.

Now arrange the circled letters to form the surprise answer, as suggested by the above cartoon.

Print the SURPRISE ANSWER here

THE

JUMBLE®

Unscramble these four Jumbles,
one letter to each square, to
form four ordinary words.

CNOTH

SOYUL

LEDENE

TARRMY

NO MORE
SEATS

WHERE YOU
MIGHT SIT.

Now arrange the circled letters
to form the surprise answer, as
suggested by the above cartoon.

Print the SURPRISE ANSWER here

IN A ⬡⬡⬡⬡⬡

16

JUMBLE®

Unscramble these four Jumbles,
one letter to each square, to
form four ordinary words.

DUGEN

YANON

HIRCUN

DILERB

Not tonight—maybe tomorrow

WHAT THE FRUSTRATED
RACEHORSE WAS
ALWAYS GETTING.

Now arrange the circled letters
to form the surprise answer, as
suggested by the above cartoon.

Print the SURPRISE ANSWER here

THE

JUMBLE®

Unscramble these four Jumbles,
one letter to each square, to
form four ordinary words.

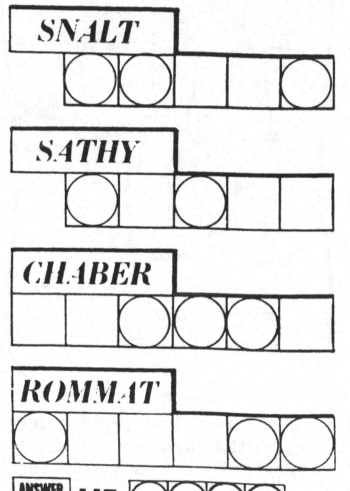

SNALT

SATHY

CHABER

ROMMAT

WHY THE UNSUCCESSFUL
TENNIS PLAYER
WAS OFFERED A
CIGARETTE LIGHTER.

Now arrange the circled letters
to form the surprise answer, as
suggested by the above cartoon.

ANSWER here HE ⭕⭕⭕⭕ ALL HIS ⭕⭕⭕⭕⭕⭕⭕⭕

JUMBLE®

Unscramble these four Jumbles, one letter to each square, to form four ordinary words.

SOMYS

CNATH

EPSOOP

MOYGOL

PALS BROKEN UP IN THE MOUNTAINS.

Now arrange the circled letters to form the surprise answer, as suggested by the above cartoon.

Print the SURPRISE ANSWER here

JUMBLE®

Unscramble these four Jumbles,
one letter to each square, to
form four ordinary words.

HIFEC

MILTI

GIANAU

MURIAB

SOUNDS LIKE A
CRIME IN CHINA.

Now arrange the circled letters
to form the surprise answer, as
suggested by the above cartoon.

Print the SURPRISE ANSWER here

JUMBLE®

Unscramble these four Jumbles, one letter to each square, to form four ordinary words.

MURYM

WARFE

SAFRAC

CLARGI

IT'S WARM WITHOUT *IT*.

Now arrange the circled letters to form the surprise answer, as suggested by the above cartoon.

Print the SURPRISE ANSWER here

JUMBLE®

Unscramble these four Jumbles, one letter to each square, to form four ordinary words.

TEAHB

YEEPA

DOULCY

EXCOIB

RAN DOWN THE BEACH.

Now arrange the circled letters to form the surprise answer, as suggested by the above cartoon.

Print the SURPRISE ANSWER here

JUMBLE®

Unscramble these four Jumbles, one letter to each square, to form four ordinary words.

EUQUE

POAKK

SLAQUL

ROTGOT

STARVATION DIET

THE EXTREMITIES ONE MIGHT REACH!

Now arrange the circled letters to form the surprise answer, as suggested by the above cartoon.

Print the SURPRISE ANSWER here

JUMBLE®

Unscramble these four Jumbles, one letter to each square, to form four ordinary words.

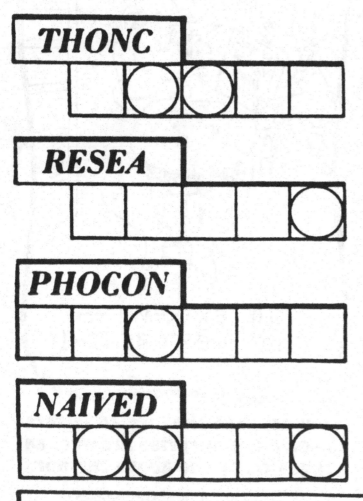

THONC

RESEA

PHOCON

NAIVED

Print the SURPRISE ANSWER here

Loser gets him!

ODDLY ENOUGH
WHAT THIS MIGHT BE !

Now arrange the circled letters to form the surprise answer, as suggested by the above cartoon.

JUMBLE®

Unscramble these four Jumbles,
one letter to each square, to
form four ordinary words.

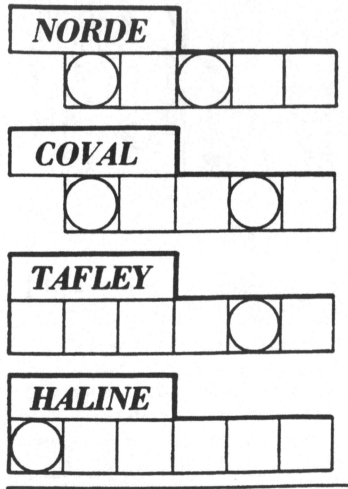

NORDE

COVAL

TAFLEY

HALINE

Print the SURPRISE ANSWER here

Oops—sorry!

IT SHOULD BE
PUT BACK ON
ITS COURSE.

Now arrange the circled letters
to form the surprise answer, as
suggested by the above cartoon.

JUMBLE®

Unscramble these four Jumbles, one letter to each square, to form four ordinary words.

SASIB

TREXE

GRECLY

CALHUN

Going to the paddock— back in a minute

SHOW

PLACE

CHECKS ON A HORSE!

Now arrange the circled letters to form the surprise answer, as suggested by the above cartoon.

Print the SURPRISE ANSWER here

JUMBLE®

Unscramble these four Jumbles,
one letter to each square, to
form four ordinary words.

NERAV

HESER

TUSJAD

MALEYS

WHAT SHE GAVE THE
MOUNTAIN CLIMBER.

Now arrange the circled letters
to form the surprise answer, as
suggested by the above cartoon.

Print the SURPRISE ANSWER here

"⬭⬭⬭⬭⬭⬭⬭"

JUMBLE.

Unscramble these four Jumbles,
one letter to each square, to
form four ordinary words.

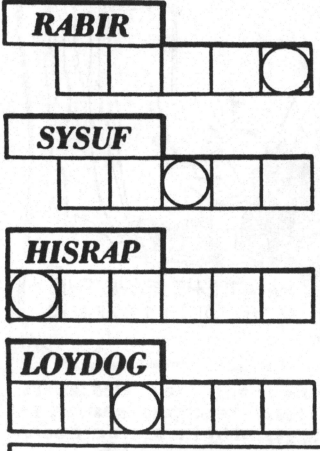

RABIR

SYSUF

HISRAP

LOYDOG

THESE ATHLETES CAN
BE EXPECTED TO START
PROSPERING

Now arrange the circled letters
to form the surprise answer, as
suggested by the above cartoon.

Print the SURPRISE ANSWER here

"  "

DAILY SPORTS JUMBLE

J

JUMBLE®

Unscramble these four Jumbles,
one letter to each square, to form
four ordinary words.

YIRDT

FETHY

JOLTES

BYRBAC

WOW!

COME IN THIS AND
YOU'LL WIN!

Now arrange the circled letters to
form the surprise answer, as suggested by the above cartoon.

Print answer here:

JUMBLE®

Unscramble these four Jumbles, one letter to each square, to form four ordinary words.

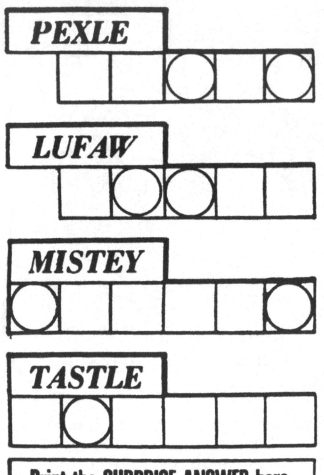

PEXLE

LUFAW

MISTEY

TASTLE

Print the SURPRISE ANSWER here

THE RUNNER SATISFIED HIS THIRST AFTER THIS.

Now arrange the circled letters to form the surprise answer, as suggested by the above cartoon.

A

JUMBLE®

Unscramble these four Jumbles, one letter to each square, to form four ordinary words.

LEWJE

DYPET

SIFOSY

BERROK

FOR THOSE WHO TRAIN BY NIGHT.

Now arrange the circled letters to form the surprise answer, as suggested by the above cartoon.

Print answer here:

JUMBLE®

Unscramble these four Jumbles,
one letter to each square, to form
four ordinary words.

KLULS

BIBAR

GANNIA

LEMPOC

Looks like a fighter!

PETS

A DOG THAT
SOUNDS LIKE A
BOXER.

Now arrange the circled letters to
form the surprise answer, as suggested by the above cartoon.

Print answer here:

JUMBLE®

Unscramble these four Jumbles, one letter to each square, to form four ordinary words.

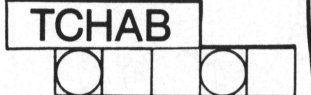

TCHAB

RAWGE

TAPECK

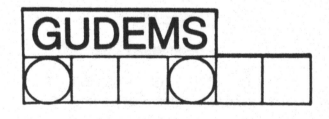

GUDEMS

Sometimes I get bored

ARCHERY MIGHT BE AN INTERESTING SPORT, BUT IT HAS THIS.

Now arrange the circled letters to form the surprise answer, as suggested by the above cartoon.

Answer here: ITS ◯◯◯◯◯◯◯◯◯◯

34

JUMBLE®

Unscramble these four Jumbles,
one letter to each square, to form
four ordinary words.

RYPOG

LUGEY

NUIJER

RUFIAN

WHERE THE SHORT
SPRINTER WAS
UNEXPECTEDLY
SUCCESSFUL.

Now arrange the circled letters to
form the surprise answer, as suggested by the above cartoon.

Print answer here: IN THE ⬡⬡⬡⬡⬡ ⬡⬡⬡

JUMBLE®

Unscramble these four Jumbles, one letter to each square, to form four ordinary words.

DUGAR

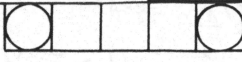

GANTE

UNBOYT

TIGBLE

STARED AT THE MOTORCYCLIST.

Now arrange the circled letters to form the surprise answer, as suggested by the above cartoon.

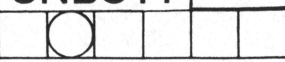

Print answer here: " ⬡⬡⬡⬡⬡⬡⬡ "

JUMBLE®

Unscramble these four Jumbles,
one letter to each square, to form
four ordinary words.

VOPER

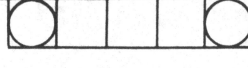

GUDOH

WHARRO

TARIPE

WHY THEY
CALLED HIM
THE CREAM OF
FIGHTERS.

Now arrange the circled letters to
form the surprise answer, as suggested by the above cartoon.

Answer: HE ⬜⬜⬜ ⬜⬜⬜⬜⬜⬜⬜

JUMBLE®

Unscramble these four Jumbles, one letter to each square, to form four ordinary words.

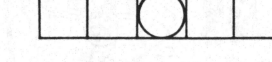
SOBAS

ALUVE

VISTEN

REBURB

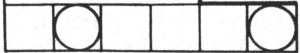
SOMETHING THAT COMES BETWEEN OPPONENTS.

FIGHTS TONITE!

Now arrange the circled letters to form the surprise answer, as suggested by the above cartoon.

Print answer here: " ⬡⬡⬡⬡⬡⬡ "

JUMBLE®

Unscramble these four Jumbles, one letter to each square, to form four ordinary words.

CUFOS

YENED

VEECAL

LUFNIX

WHAT SHE THOUGHT THE DEFENSIVE BACK WAS.

Now arrange the circled letters to form the surprise answer, as suggested by the above cartoon.

Answer here: VERY

JUMBLE®

Unscramble these four Jumbles, one letter to each square, to form four ordinary words.

NUNAL

OAPIN

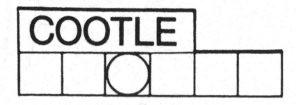

COOTLE

RANOUD

SKIING IS A SPORT IN WHICH SOME END UP THIS WAY.

Now arrange the circled letters to form the surprise answer, as suggested by the above cartoon.

Print answer here:

40

JUMBLE.

Unscramble these four Jumbles,
one letter to each square, to form
four ordinary words.

LIVIG

BLERY

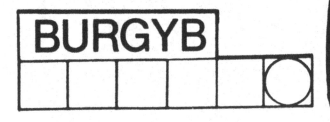

BURGYB

HALMYN

Wish I
were as
good as
you

MIGHT BE FOUND
AMONG MEN VYING
WITH EACH OTHER.

Now arrange the circled letters to
form the surprise answer, as suggested by the above cartoon.

Print answer here:

JUMBLE®

Unscramble these four Jumbles,
one letter to each square, to form
four ordinary words.

VUCER

NOFEL

LAFBLE

CALPEA

You'll have to
shape up

WHEN HE TOOK THAT
COURSE IN MARINE
BIOLOGY HIS
GRADES WERE THIS.

Now arrange the circled letters to
form the surprise answer, as suggested by the above cartoon.

Print answer here: BELOW "◯" ◯◯◯◯◯

JUMBLE.

Unscramble these four Jumbles,
one letter to each square, to form
four ordinary words.

BISCA

HOYNE

DEXOUS

LAGYAX

WHAT THE GIRLS
SAID THAT HANDSOME
SPRINTER WAS.

Now arrange the circled letters to
form the surprise answer, as suggested by the above cartoon.

Print answer here: " ⬡⬡⬡⬡⬡⬡⬡ !"

JUMBLE®

Unscramble these four Jumbles, one letter to each square, to form four ordinary words.

HACTY

TOSOP

AMRUTE

COPILY

Must have taken lots of working out

FROM ATHLETICS ONE COULD ACHIEVE THIS.

Now arrange the circled letters to form the surprise answer, as suggested by the above cartoon.

Answer here: " ◯◯◯◯◯ ◯◯◯◯ "

JUMBLE.

Unscramble these four Jumbles, one letter to each square, to form four ordinary words.

YEVAH

TAMID

YURTIP

INKELT

Not a drop of rain in sight

CRACK!

THE ONLY REALLY RELIABLE WEATHER "REPORT."

Now arrange the circled letters to form the surprise answer, as suggested by the above cartoon.

Print answer here:

JUMBLE®

Unscramble these four Jumbles, one letter to each square, to form four ordinary words.

PYLAP

HARCI

TRIVED

NUHRGY

WHAT KIND OF YOUNGSTER DOES BASKETBALL USUALLY ATTRACT?

Now arrange the circled letters to form the surprise answer, as suggested by the above cartoon.

Answer here: A VERY ⬡⬡⬡⬡ ⬡⬡⬡⬡

JUMBLE®

Unscramble these four Jumbles,
one letter to each square, to form
four ordinary words.

AYLIG

PANCO

KADMAS

NAHMLY

A GIRL WITH
HORSE SENSE
KNOWS WHEN TO
DO THIS.

Now arrange the circled letters to
form the surprise answer, as suggested by the above cartoon.

Print answer here: ☐☐☐ " ☐☐☐ "

47

JUMBLE®

Unscramble these four Jumbles,
one letter to each square, to form
four ordinary words.

SHURC

KNEWA

BOPISH

FITONY

HE'S THE MOST IM—
PORTANT MAN IN THE
RING BECAUSE HE'S
THE ONLY ONE —

Now arrange the circled letters to
form the surprise answer, as suggested by the above cartoon.

Print answer here:

JUMBLE®

Unscramble these four Jumbles, one letter to each square, to form four ordinary words.

INSIF

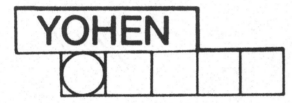

YOHEN

KOHOED

UNTEAB

He's got muscles between his ears, too

WHERE THE CONCEITED WEIGHT LIFTER LET HIS BODY GO.

Now arrange the circled letters to form the surprise answer, as suggested by the above cartoon.

Answer here:

JUMBLE®

Unscramble these four Jumbles, one letter to each square, to form four ordinary words.

KWONN

SELLI

ODUXTE

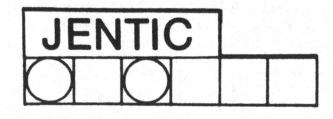

JENTIC

WHAT HE BLAMED HIS BAD LUCK ON.

Now arrange the circled letters to form the surprise answer, as suggested by the above cartoon.

Answer: A ⬡⬡⬡⬡ AT THE ⬡⬡⬡⬡⬡

JUMBLE®

Unscramble these four Jumbles, one letter to each square, to form four ordinary words.

RORYS

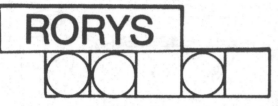

HERBT

SULTYS

RUGBBY

WHAT THE MAN WHO WAS RUNNING IN SHORT BURSTS ENDED UP WITH.

Now arrange the circled letters to form the surprise answer, as suggested by the above cartoon.

Answer: ⬡⬡⬡⬡⬡ ⬡⬡⬡⬡⬡⬡

JUMBLE.

Unscramble these four Jumbles,
one letter to each square, to form
four ordinary words.

NELEK

BROEP

TERVOX

CAYGLE

WHAT YOU MIGHT
EXPECT A POOL-
PLAYING THIEF
TO DO.

Now arrange the circled letters to
form the surprise answer, as suggested by the above cartoon.

Answer: ⬡⬡⬡⬡⬡⬡ THE ⬡⬡⬡⬡

JUMBLE®

Unscramble these four Jumbles,
one letter to each square, to form
four ordinary words.

NIGVY

GANOW

MELING

STINCH

EXIT

WHAT THE NEAR-
SIGHTED BOXER HAD
TROUBLE FINDING.

Now arrange the circled letters to
form the surprise answer, as suggested by the above cartoon.

Answer here: THE " ◯◯◯◯◯◯ - ◯◯ "

JUMBLE.

Unscramble these four Jumbles,
one letter to each square, to form
four ordinary words.

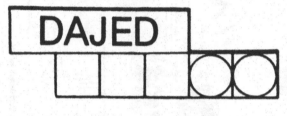

DAJED

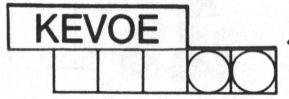

KEVOE

ONE CAT TOLD
THE OTHER TO BE
CAREFUL LEST
HE DO THIS.

BARNEY

CLITIE

Now arrange the circled letters to
form the surprise answer, as suggested by the above cartoon.

Answer: ⟨○○○⟩ UP IN THAT ⟨○○○○○○⟩

JUMBLE®

Unscramble these four Jumbles, one letter to each square, to form four ordinary words.

MIRGE

INAFT

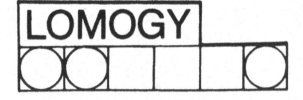

LOMOGY

RUGEDD

THE COFFEE TYCOON DECIDED TO RETIRE BECAUSE HE COULDN'T STAND THIS.

Now arrange the circled letters to form the surprise answer, as suggested by the above cartoon.

Answer: THE [ ][ ][ ][ ][ ] " [ ][ ][ ][ ][ ] "

JUMBLE®

Unscramble these four Jumbles, one letter to each square, to form four ordinary words.

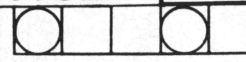

WYSEN

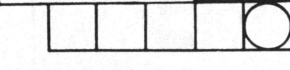

CONOR

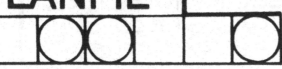

LANFIE

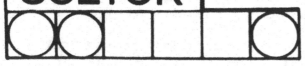

SCETOK

WHEN JUNIOR SEEMED TO BE SPENDING TOO MUCH TIME READING POETRY, THIS IS WHAT DAD FINALLY SAID.

Now arrange the circled letters to form the surprise answer, as suggested by the above cartoon.

Answer: "  ,  ? "

56

JUMBLE.

Unscramble these four Jumbles,
one letter to each square, to form
four ordinary words.

THEFC

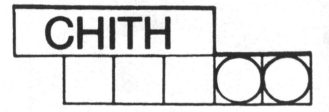

CHITH

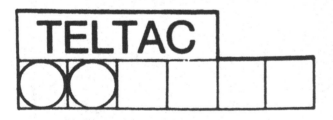

TELTAC

RAYPOD

Next!

WHAT THEY CALLED
THE TEAM'S
PSYCHIATRIST.

Now arrange the circled letters to
form the surprise answer, as suggested by the above cartoon.

Answer: THE "⬡⬡⬡⬡" ⬡⬡⬡⬡⬡

JUMBLE.®

Unscramble these four Jumbles, one letter to each square, to form four ordinary words.

DAGEA

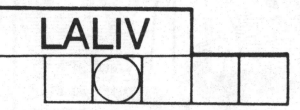

LALIV

LYMBAC

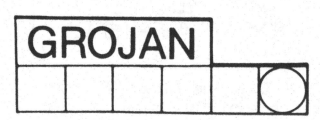

GROJAN

Hey, Boss—you should have been a pro

A HYPOCRITE IS SOMEONE WHO CAN'T TELL THE TRUTH WITH-OUT DOING THIS.

Now arrange the circled letters to form the surprise answer, as suggested by the above cartoon.

Print answer here:

JUMBLE®

Unscramble these four Jumbles,
one letter to each square, to form
four ordinary words.

CIMEN

ANAFU

RETHOX

FORPIT

Tee hee

WHAT THE STAR
PITCHER TURNED
BOXER ENDED
UP AS.

Now arrange the circled letters to
form the surprise answer, as suggested by the above cartoon.

Answer here: A " □□ - □□□□□□ "

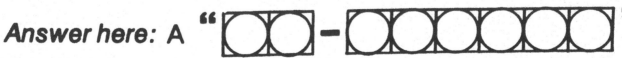

JUMBLE.

Unscramble these four Jumbles,
one letter to each square, to form
four ordinary words.

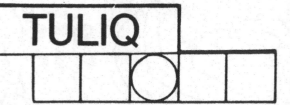

TULIQ

ARZYC

GALEEB

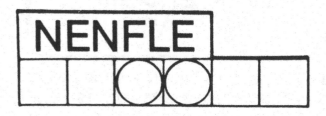

NENFLE

COMING CLOSER—
COULD IT BE
"IN RANGE"?

Now arrange the circled letters to
form the surprise answer, as suggested by the above cartoon.

Print answer here: "  "

(Answers tomorrow)

JUMBLE®

Unscramble these four Jumbles, one letter to each square, to form four ordinary words.

GEMID

BOMUG

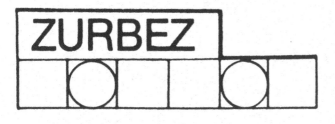

ZURBEZ

LAMORN

WHAT THE COACH DID EVERY TIME A PLAYER FUMBLED.

Now arrange the circled letters to form the surprise answer, as suggested by the above cartoon.

Print answer here:

JUMBLE®

Unscramble these four Jumbles, one letter to each square, to form four ordinary words.

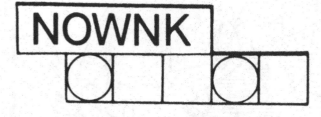

NOWNK

RONED

TOYBAN

SEPPIN

WHAT SKIERS GET INSTEAD OF ATHLETE'S FOOT.

Now arrange the circled letters to form the surprise answer, as suggested by the above cartoon.

Print answer here:

JUMBLE®

Unscramble these four Jumbles, one letter to each square, to form four ordinary words.

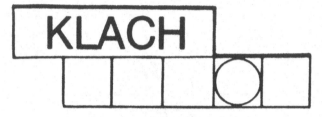

KLACH

METHY

FLOAFY

TANIED

SKIING IS A WINTERTIME SPORT OFTEN LEARNED THUS.

Now arrange the circled letters to form the surprise answer, as suggested by the above cartoon.

Answer here:  "  "

JUMBLE.

Unscramble these four Jumbles, one letter to each square, to form four ordinary words.

YOHBB

TOPIL

GIPNAY

FYLLAT

WHAT'S A BALL HIT HIGH IN THE AIR DURING A GAME PLAYED AFTER DARK?

Now arrange the circled letters to form the surprise answer, as suggested by the above cartoon.

Answer: A ⬡⬡⬡⬡ - ⬡⬡ - ⬡⬡⬡⬡⬡⬡

JUMBLE®

Unscramble these four Jumbles, one letter to each square, to form four ordinary words.

WADAR

TELOX

KOECIO

EXNOST

WHAT HAPPENED WHEN THAT BODY BUILDER PUT A TIGHT T-SHIRT ON HIS TORSO?

Now arrange the circled letters to form the surprise answer, as suggested by the above cartoon.

Print answer here:

JUMBLE.

Unscramble these four Jumbles,
one letter to each square, to form
four ordinary words.

ESTAE

BOAVE

REPERF

CAULNY

WHAT SOME
WRESTLING
IS A FORM OF.

Now arrange the circled letters to
form the surprise answer, as suggested by the above cartoon.

Answer: [ ] " [ ] "

JUMBLE®

Unscramble these four Jumbles,
one letter to each square, to form
four ordinary words.

POVER

THOLC

CRASAF

TREEMP

WHAT THAT TV
SHOW ABOUT SKIING
TURNED OUT TO BE.

Now arrange the circled letters to
form the surprise answer, as suggested by the above cartoon.

Answer: A "⟨◯◯◯◯◯⟩" ⟨◯◯◯◯◯⟩

JUMBLE.

Unscramble these four Jumbles, one letter to each square, to form four ordinary words.

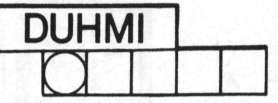

DUHMI

KANTE

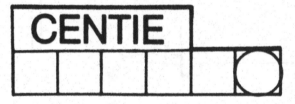

CENTIE

SUCCAU

ENTER THE $1,000,000 LOTTERY TODAY!!

A GUY WHO LEAVES TOO MUCH TO CHANCE USUALLY HASN'T GOT THIS.

Now arrange the circled letters to form the surprise answer, as suggested by the above cartoon.

Print answer here:

JUMBLE.

Unscramble these four Jumbles,
one letter to each square, to form
four ordinary words.

TAHBE

KROPE

RUQUOM

TUCSOC

Missed
again!

WHAT A DUCK
HUNTER MIGHT BE.

Now arrange the circled letters to
form the surprise answer, as suggested by the above cartoon.

Answer: A "⬡⬡⬡⬡⬡" ⬡⬡⬡⬡

JUMBLE.

Unscramble these four Jumbles, one letter to each square, to form four ordinary words.

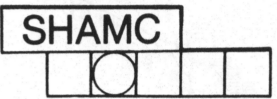

SHAMC

CROFE

PAMERC

NUTTAR

HE WAS HOPING TO GET HIS TRIM FIGURE BACK, BUT ACTUALLY HAD THIS.

Now arrange the circled letters to form the surprise answer, as suggested by the above cartoon.

Answer here: A

70

JUMBLE.

Unscramble these four Jumbles, one letter to each square, to form four ordinary words.

CELER

DEEXU

ARMKUP

PRAULB

A BIRD HE SHOULD HAVE THOUGHT OF BEFORE HE WAS KNOCKED OUT.

Now arrange the circled letters to form the surprise answer, as suggested by the above cartoon.

Print answer here:

71

JUMBLE®

Unscramble these four Jumbles,
one letter to each square, to form
four ordinary words.

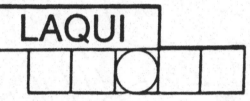

LAQUI

HEWIG

ENGRYT

NEWECH

Lucky shot

WHAT THE TYCOON
CONSIDERED HIS
WINNING POINT.

Now arrange the circled letters to
form the surprise answer, as suggested by the above cartoon.

Print answer here: A

JUMBLE.

Unscramble these four Jumbles,
one letter to each square, to form
four ordinary words.

ANKEW

NEFTO

BLACOT

SLUIBY

Sign here

WHAT KIND
OF INSURANCE
POLICY SHOULD A
SKIER TAKE OUT?

Now arrange the circled letters to
form the surprise answer, as suggested by the above cartoon.

Answer: A "☐☐☐☐☐ — ☐☐☐☐☐☐" ONE

JUMBLE.

Unscramble these four Jumbles,
one letter to each square, to form
four ordinary words.

KNALB

ENKLE

FLUDON

TORFOG

BEGINNING HORSE-
BACK RIDERS OFTEN
DO IT THIS WAY.

Now arrange the circled letters to
form the surprise answer, as suggested by the above cartoon.

Print answer here:

JUMBLE®

Unscramble these four Jumbles,
one letter to each square, to form
four ordinary words.

LITAP

TUSIE

JITNEC

SPRAYT

After all I went
through to—

THE MOST BRUTAL
ASPECT OF BOXING
THESE DAYS.

Now arrange the circled letters to
form the surprise answer, as suggested by the above cartoon.

Answer: THE ⬡⬡⬡⬡⬡⬡ OF ⬡⬡⬡⬡⬡

JUMBLE.

Unscramble these four Jumbles,
one letter to each square, to form
four ordinary words.

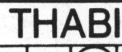

THABI
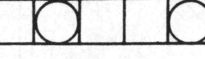

SUAPE

RAHBOR

DRENGE

We're the best!

WHAT THOSE
SNOBBISH MEMBERS
OF THE HORSEY SET
THOUGHT THEY WERE.

Now arrange the circled letters to
form the surprise answer, as suggested by the above cartoon.

Answer here: A

JUMBLE.

Unscramble these four Jumbles, one letter to each square, to form four ordinary words.

PIRGE

HUTOM
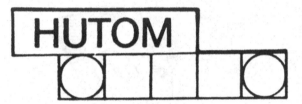

SPUGMY

REBUPS

WHAT SMALL SLED DOGS ARE CALLED.

Now arrange the circled letters to form the surprise answer, as suggested by the above cartoon.

Answer: "⬭⬭⬭⬭" ⬭⬭⬭⬭⬭⬭⬭⬭

JUMBLE®

Unscramble these four Jumbles,
one letter to each square, to form
four ordinary words.

VEFER

SNABI

TEACKS

BELTOG

I've got my retirement
all figured out

THE BEST
THING TO SAVE
FOR OLD AGE.

Now arrange the circled letters to
form the surprise answer, as suggested by the above cartoon.

Print answer here:

JUMBLE®

Unscramble these four Jumbles,
one letter to each square, to form
four ordinary words.

VOGEL

Pay you later

FELCT

TUSACC

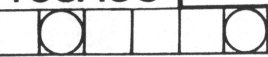

DOAFER

WHAT THE RUNNER'S
DIET CONSISTED
OF, NATURALLY.

Now arrange the circled letters to
form the surprise answer, as suggested by the above cartoon.

Print answer here:

JUMBLE.

Unscramble these four Jumbles,
one letter to each square, to form
four ordinary words.

RILLT

YADDD

WHOALL

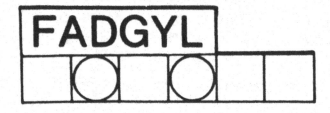

FADGYL

Wow! Some shot!

SOUNDS LIKE A
PRETTY GOOD
DISTANCE ON THE
GOLF COURSE.

Now arrange the circled letters to
form the surprise answer, as suggested by the above cartoon.

Print answer here: A "◯◯◯◯ ◯◯◯"

80

JUMBLE.

Unscramble these four Jumbles,
one letter to each square, to form
four ordinary words.

WALBY

REGIM

PINKAD

BOLUDE

Well, dear—how
did it go?

WHAT A GAME
OF GOLF
SOMETIMES IS.

Now arrange the circled letters to
form the surprise answer, as suggested by the above cartoon.

Answer: A
GOOD ⬚⬚⬚⬚⬚ ⬚⬚⬚⬚⬚⬚

JUMBLE.

Unscramble these four Jumbles, one letter to each square, to form four ordinary words.

YABBE

THRAW

YECKAL

ACTUFE

He should hit the books more often

WHAT THE HALFBACK WAS IN HIS CLASSROOM WORK.

Now arrange the circled letters to form the surprise answer, as suggested by the above cartoon.

Print answer here:

JUMBLE.

Unscramble these four Jumbles, one letter to each square, to form four ordinary words.

THECK

HIWSS

BROTED

CRIONI

WHAT THE FISHERMAN TURNED TV EXECUTIVE KNEW HOW TO MAKE.

Now arrange the circled letters to form the surprise answer, as suggested by the above cartoon.

Answer here: THE "◯◯◯" ◯◯◯◯

JUMBLE.

Unscramble these four Jumbles,
one letter to each square, to form
four ordinary words.

HOUTY

YIPTE

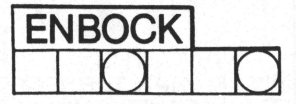

ENBOCK

SUFOAM

GYM

WHAT TO
EXERCISE WHEN
YOU FEEL YOU'RE
PUTTING ON WEIGHT.

Now arrange the circled letters to
form the surprise answer, as suggested by the above cartoon.

Print answer here:

JUMBLE.

Unscramble these four Jumbles,
one letter to each square, to form
four ordinary words.

MUJYP

NAPOR

DRENER

NAMMAD

For once I played like a pro

WHAT THE
GOLF ADDICT'S
CHILDREN CALLED
THEIR FATHER.

Now arrange the circled letters to
form the surprise answer, as suggested by the above cartoon.

Print answer here: "☐◯◯◯ – ◯◯◯☐"

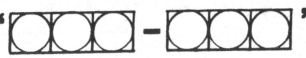

JUMBLE.

Unscramble these four Jumbles,
one letter to each square, to form
four ordinary words.

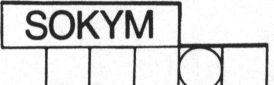

SOKYM

DYSIA

TOSFRY

FLUTIP

WHAT ICE IS.

Now arrange the circled letters to
form the surprise answer, as suggested by the above cartoon.

Answer here: "  "

JUMBLE®

Unscramble these four Jumbles,
one letter to each square, to form
four ordinary words.

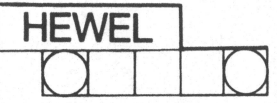

HEWEL

TULSY

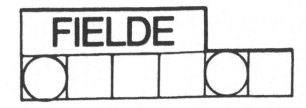

NEBATE

FIELDE

WHAT JUNIOR SAID
ABOUT THE GAME,
AFTER MOM MADE
HIM A NEW BASE-
BALL UNIFORM.

Now arrange the circled letters to
form the surprise answer, as suggested by the above cartoon.

Answer: IT'S ⬡⬡⬡ "⬡⬡⬡⬡⬡" UP

JUMBLE.

Unscramble these four Jumbles,
one letter to each square, to form
four ordinary words.

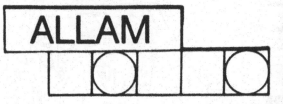

ALLAM

GRUPE

MINKOO

FLAMEE

WHAT THE
BASEBALL THAT HIT
THE DENTIST'S
OFFICE WAS.

Now arrange the circled letters to
form the surprise answer, as suggested by the above cartoon.

Answer: THE " ⬚⬚⬚⬚ " ⬚⬚⬚⬚⬚⬚⬚

JUMBLE.

Unscramble these four Jumbles, one letter to each square, to form four ordinary words.

IDDEA

ARZYC

CARNID

TICEXE

WHAT THEY DID WHEN THAT MAN FELL OFF THE HORSE.

Now arrange the circled letters to form the surprise answer, as suggested by the above cartoon.

Answer here: "  -  " HIM

JUMBLE.

Unscramble these four Jumbles,
one letter to each square, to form
four ordinary words.

YARPH

NAPAG

JOOUSY

CATATH

HEALTH SALON
BAR | WE GET RID OF THAT LARD | BARGAIN

WHAT THEY
CALLED THAT SKID
ROW GYM.

Now arrange thé circled letters to
form the surprise answer, as suggested by the above cartoon.

Answer: THE " ◯◯◯◯◯◯ " ◯◯◯◯

JUMBLE®

Unscramble these four Jumbles,
one letter to each square, to form
four ordinary words.

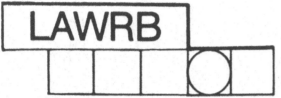
LAWRB

INHEW

MARROD

SYPEDE

FOR A CONSCIENTIOUS
DIETER THIS SHOULD
BE SUFFICIENT.

Now arrange the circled letters to
form the surprise answer, as suggested by the above cartoon.

Answer: A ⬡⬡⬡⬡ TO THE "⬡⬡⬡⬡⬡"

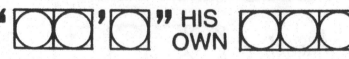

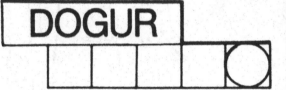

JUMBLE.

Unscramble these four Jumbles, one letter to each square, to form four ordinary words.

SYSUF

DOGUR

JOADIN

SMARDI

You might want to clean your room first

Are you kidding?!

WHAT A SPOILED BRAT DOES.

Now arrange the circled letters to form the surprise answer, as suggested by the above cartoon.

Print answer here: "◯◯'◯" HIS OWN ◯◯◯

JUMBLE®

Unscramble these four Jumbles,
one letter to each square, to form
four ordinary words.

FEACH

NORDE

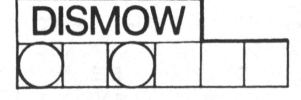

DISMOW

TIRRAY

Sunny all day

HE'S SOMETIMES
WEATHER-WISE, BUT
MORE OFTEN THIS.

Now arrange the circled letters to
form the surprise answer, as suggested by the above cartoon.

Print answer here:

JUMBLE.

Unscramble these four Jumbles,
one letter to each square, to form
four ordinary words.

HOYNE

MERIC

GLEMIT

DROWBY

Let's go!

3-16

WHAT SHE THOUGHT
WHEN SHE SWITCHED
FROM HIGH HEELS
TO SNEAKERS.

Now arrange the circled letters to
form the surprise answer, as suggested by the above cartoon.

Answer: "IT'S A 〇〇〇 〇〇〇〇〇〇〇〇 "

JUMBLE.

Unscramble these four Jumbles, one letter to each square, to form four ordinary words.

YENEM

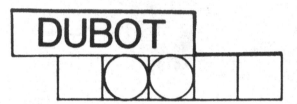

DUBOT

GINTRY

UNDASE

START

WHAT A GUY WHO PAYS TO ENTER THE MARATHON IS SURE TO GET.

Now arrange the circled letters to form the surprise answer, as suggested by the above cartoon.

Answer here: A  FOR HIS

JUMBLE®

Unscramble these four Jumbles,
one letter to each square, to form
four ordinary words.

DOLOB

KYASH

TRAVOC

MOYLOG

HE WON THE
BIGGEST BET AT THE
GREYHOUND RACE
BECAUSE HE
HAD THIS.

Now arrange the circled letters to
form the surprise answer, as suggested by the above cartoon.

Print answer here: A " ⬡⬡⬡ " ⬡⬡⬡

96

JUMBLE.

Unscramble these four Jumbles,
one letter to each square, to form
four ordinary words.

VENET

OONES

NERKUB

SHURTH

No wonder
he's number
one!

And all
those
commercials!

THEY WERE IN
THE MILLIONS!

Now arrange the circled letters to
form the surprise answer, as suggested by the above cartoon.

Answer here: HIS ☐☐☐ ☐☐☐☐☐☐☐

JUMBLE.

Unscramble these four Jumbles, one letter to each square, to form four ordinary words.

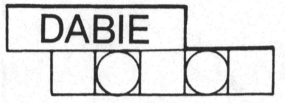

DABIE

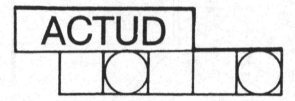

ACTUD

ROYLOP

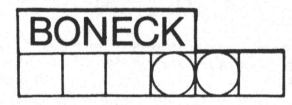

BONECK

Looks like we're going to have great fishing

Don't bet on it

WHAT THE SKEPTIC'S OUTLOOK IS.

Now arrange the circled letters to form the surprise answer, as suggested by the above cartoon.

Answer here: A "☐☐☐☐☐ ☐☐☐☐"

98

JUMBLE.

Unscramble these four Jumbles,
one letter to each square, to form
four ordinary words.

VOGEL

KRIHE

INNACE

GOHBUT

WHAT THE NUDIST
CAMP'S STAR
ATHLETE RAN A
HUNDRED YARDS IN.

Now arrange the circled letters to
form the surprise answer, as suggested by the above cartoon.

Print answer here:

JUMBLE.

Unscramble these four Jumbles, one letter to each square, to form four ordinary words.

THEIG

ISTOC

HANEEV

GLEINT

A HORSE IS WHAT MORE PEOPLE BET ON---

Now arrange the circled letters to form the surprise answer, as suggested by the above cartoon.

Print answer here:

JUMBLE.

Unscramble these four Jumbles,
one letter to each square, to form
four ordinary words.

BREYD

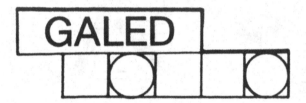

GALED

DINCAR

SMUCLY

WHAT HE HOPED
THIS EXERCISE
WOULD DO TO
HIS BODY FAT.

Now arrange the circled letters to
form the surprise answer, as suggested by the above cartoon.

Print answer here:  IT

JUMBLE.

Unscramble these four Jumbles,
one letter to each square, to form
four ordinary words.

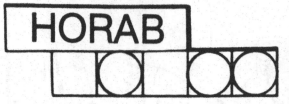

HORAB

CUFOS

ASHRIP

KLAYEC

SHE KNEW HER
HUSBAND LIKE
A BOOK---

Now arrange the circled letters to
form the surprise answer, as suggested by the above cartoon.

Answer here: A "⬡⬡⬡⬡⬡" ⬡⬡⬡⬡

102

JUMBLE®

Unscramble these four Jumbles,
one letter to each square, to form
four ordinary words.

CONIT

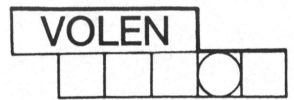

VOLEN

ZERBAL

REFTER

THE MANAGER
SAID THE PINCH
HITTER WOULD BE
A CHANGE---

Now arrange the circled letters to
form the surprise answer, as suggested by the above cartoon.

Answer: ◯◯◯ THE "◯◯◯◯◯◯"

JUMBLE.

Unscramble these four Jumbles,
one letter to each square, to form
four ordinary words.

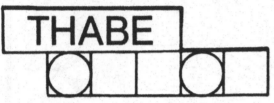

THABE

YUHRR

DELPOW

RANCAL

WHERE THE HEAVY-
WEIGHT CHAMPIONSHIP
WAS HELD.

Now arrange the circled letters to
form the surprise answer, as suggested by the above cartoon.

Answer: AT THE " ⬡⬡⬡⬡⬡ ⬡⬡⬡⬡ "

JUMBLE.

Unscramble these four Jumbles, one letter to each square, to form four ordinary words.

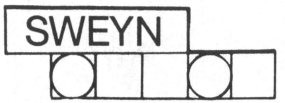

SWEYN

OSOGE

DEECES

BEHREY

Watch what you say in this crowd

WHAT IT TAKES TO "BRIDLE" ONE'S TONGUE.

Now arrange the circled letters to form the surprise answer, as suggested by the above cartoon.

Answer here:

105

JUMBLE.

Unscramble these four Jumbles, one letter to each square, to form four ordinary words.

GOSUB

MOROG

WHAT THE FORMER BODYBUILDER'S TORSO BECAME AS HE REACHED MIDDLE AGE.

RAYPER

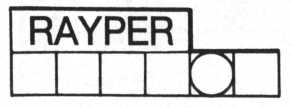
MORRET

Now arrange the circled letters to form the surprise answer, as suggested by the above cartoon.

Print answer here:

106

JUMBLE®

Unscramble these four Jumbles,
one letter to each square, to form
four ordinary words.

PYDET

THEFC

RAPOUR

NESHCO

THE LESS ONE KNOWS
OF BOXING, THE MORE
ONE BECOMES AC-
QUAINTED WITH THIS.

Now arrange the circled letters to
form the surprise answer, as suggested by the above cartoon.

Print answer here:

JUMBLE.

Unscramble these four Jumbles, one letter to each square, to form four ordinary words.

TACUE

KROOB

NUPWOT

ENKASH

You don't look well

STRIKE THREE!

HOW THE BALL-PLAYER FELT ON AN OFF DAY.

Now arrange the circled letters to form the surprise answer, as suggested by the above cartoon.

Answer here: ⬡⬡⬡ OF "⬡⬡⬡⬡⬡"

JUMBLE®

Unscramble these four Jumbles, one letter to each square, to form four ordinary words.

DEVEL

KIHCT

ACCUST

CLARIA

WHAT HAPPENED TO THE HORSE NAMED "POISON IVY"?

Now arrange the circled letters to form the surprise answer, as suggested by the above cartoon.

Answer: IT WAS " ⬭⬭⬭⬭⬭⬭⬭⬭⬭⬭ "

JUMBLE.

Unscramble these four Jumbles, one letter to each square, to form four ordinary words.

YAFFT

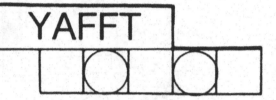

TEAGA

ZENFRY

WILDEM

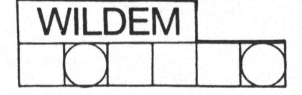

WHAT THAT GOLF FANATIC HAD IN HIS EYES.

Now arrange the circled letters to form the surprise answer, as suggested by the above cartoon.

Answer here: A "◯◯◯◯◯◯◯" LOOK

JUMBLE.

Unscramble these four Jumbles,
one letter to each square, to form
four ordinary words.

GYTAN

YIZZD

LESTUS

YONIFT

HOW PEOPLE LEARN
ICE-SKATING.

Now arrange the circled letters to
form the surprise answer, as suggested by the above cartoon.

Answer: IN SEVERAL " ☐☐☐☐☐☐☐☐ "
SEVERAL

JUMBLE.

Unscramble these four Jumbles,
one letter to each square, to form
four ordinary words.

UGIED

HIFAT

ALBBED

CORNBO

Why doesn't he grow up?

SOME THOUGHT THE
BASKETBALL PLAYER
WAS ACTING LIKE A
BABY WHEN HE
WAS DOING THIS.

Now arrange the circled letters to
form the surprise answer, as suggested by the above cartoon.

Answer here: " ◯◯◯◯◯◯◯◯◯ "

JUMBLE®

Unscramble these four Jumbles, one letter to each square, to form four ordinary words.

FAHFC

OMIDI

CURPSE

THELME

THE PRIZEFIGHTER WOKE UP AND FOUND THIS.

Now arrange the circled letters to form the surprise answer, as suggested by the above cartoon.

Answer here:

JUMBLE.

Unscramble these four Jumbles, one letter to each square, to form four ordinary words.

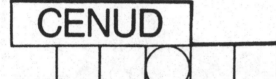

CENUD

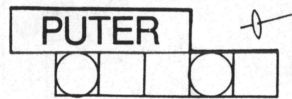

PUTER

DAILIN

THORUG

SKIING IS A SPORT IN WHICH MANY END UP----

Now arrange the circled letters to form the surprise answer, as suggested by the above cartoon.

Print answer here: "  "

114

JUMBLE.

Unscramble these four Jumbles,
one letter to each square, to form
four ordinary words.

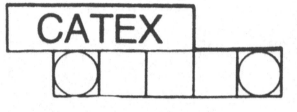

CATEX

NELLK

RAMPHE

YECKAL

IN GOLF, THE BALL
SELDOM LIES AS
WELL AS THIS.

Now arrange the circled letters to
form the surprise answer, as suggested by the above cartoon.

Answer here:

115

JUMBLE.

Unscramble these four Jumbles,
one letter to each square, to form
four ordinary words.

YULST

ROHTT

MIULEH

TAIREW

HOW THE FORMER
FOOTBALL PLAYER
NOW DOES MOST
OF HIS KICKING.

Now arrange the circled letters to
form the surprise answer, as suggested by the above cartoon.

 Answer here: ⟨ ◯◯◯◯ ⟩ HIS ⟨ ◯◯◯◯◯ ⟩

JUMBLE.

Unscramble these four Jumbles, one letter to each square, to form four ordinary words.

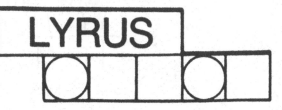

LYRUS

TOAPI

FALLUW

ALLTOW

Great shot--for a beginner

Gulp!

OVERPRAISE NEVER HURTS UNLESS YOU DO THIS.

Now arrange the circled letters to form the surprise answer, as suggested by the above cartoon.

Print answer here:

JUMBLE.

Unscramble these four Jumbles,
one letter to each square, to form
four ordinary words.

TEWCI

FYNAC

LAPEAT

REHIFE

WHAT THEY SHOUTED
WHEN HIS FEET WERE
THE FIRST TO CROSS
THE FINISH LINE.

Now arrange the circled letters to
form the surprise answer, as suggested by the above cartoon.

Answer here: ◯◯◯◯ ◯ "◯◯◯◯"!

118

JUMBLE.

Unscramble these four Jumbles,
one letter to each square, to form
four ordinary words.

SWENY

NALAC

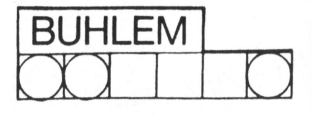

BUHLEM

TURGED

What happened to him?

WHERE THE PLAYER
WHO CARRIES THE
BALL IS USUALLY
FOUND.

Now arrange the circled letters to
form the surprise answer, as suggested by the above cartoon.

Answer here:

119

#118

JUMBLE®

Unscramble these four Jumbles, one letter to each square, to form four ordinary words.

BUMIE

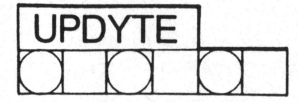

NIXEV

UPDYTE

SMALEY

Let's turn this thing around
MGR.
THAT BALLTEAM HAS BEEN IN THE CELLAR SO LONG---

Now arrange the circled letters to form the surprise answer, as suggested by the above cartoon.

Print answer here: ◯◯'◯ ◯◯◯◯◯

JUMBLE.

Unscramble these four Jumbles, one letter to each square, to form four ordinary words.

COUNE

GORAC

TOPECK

WHAT THE CURIOUS MOUNTAIN CLIMBER WANTED TO TAKE.

MEEDER

Now arrange the circled letters to form the surprise answer, as suggested by the above cartoon.

Answer: [ ][ ][ ][ ] [ ][ ][ ][ ][ ] "[ ][ ][ ][ ]"

JUMBLE.

Unscramble these four Jumbles,
one letter to each square, to form
four ordinary words.

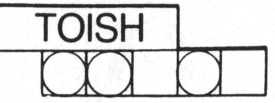

TOISH

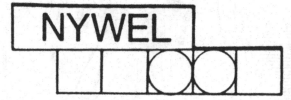

NYWEL

RESAIT

SORRAY

He and his
so-called
"free advice"

SOMETHING THAT
COSTS NOTHING IS
OFTEN THIS.

Now arrange the circled letters to
form the surprise answer, as suggested by the above cartoon.

Answer here: "◯◯◯◯◯ ◯◯◯◯"

JUMBLE.

Unscramble these four Jumbles, one letter to each square, to form four ordinary words.

DYRIT

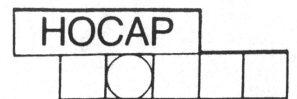

HOCAP

RENUNG

NACUNE

SHE FELL IN LOVE WITH A JOGGER WHICH MAY BE WHY SHE GOT THIS.

Now arrange the circled letters to form the surprise answer, as suggested by the above cartoon.

Answer here: THE

JUMBLE®

Unscramble these four Jumbles,
one letter to each square, to form
four ordinary words.

SIPOU

FRADT

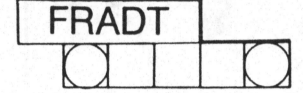

GONEPS

ROBRAW

MAY I HAVE A BASEBALL
GLOVE FOR MY SON?

SORRY

Now arrange the circled letters to
form the surprise answer, as suggested by the above cartoon.

Answer here: " WE ⬡⬡⬡⬡ '⬡ ⬡⬡⬡⬡⬡ "

JUMBLE®

Unscramble these four Jumbles, one letter to each square, to form four ordinary words.

CLOON

LESOO

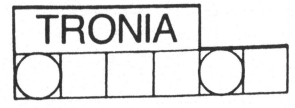

EDGERD

TRONIA

THE GOOD OLD' DAYS SEEM SO APPEALING, BECAUSE MOST OF US WERE NEITHER THIS AT THAT TIME.

Now arrange the circled letters to form the surprise answer, as suggested by the above cartoon.

Answer: "⬡⬡⬡⬡" ⬡⬡⬡ "⬡⬡⬡"

JUMBLE®

Unscramble these four Jumbles, one letter to each square, to form four ordinary words.

KUFLE

POKAK

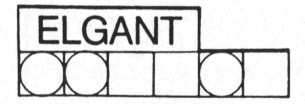

ELGANT

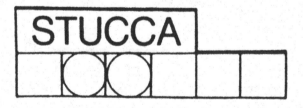

STUCCA

FOOTBALL TRYOUTS

HE BROUGHT HIS FISHING GEAR, BE-CAUSE HE HEARD THEY WERE LOOKING FOR THIS.

Now arrange the circled letters to form the surprise answer, as suggested by the above cartoon.

Print answer here:

JUMBLE.

Unscramble these four Jumbles,
one letter to each square, to form
four ordinary words.

SASEY

HIGEW

ONASAT

SPLEET

Was anyone there?

IN ORDER TO INCREASE
THE SIZE OF THE
FISH YOU CATCH,
THERE SHOULD NEVER
BE THIS.

Now arrange the circled letters to
form the surprise answer, as suggested by the above cartoon.

Print answer here:

JUMBLE.

Unscramble these four Jumbles,
one letter to each square, to form
four ordinary words.

Unbelievable!

NOFET
□ □ ◯ ◯ □

VOFAR
□ ◯ □ ◯ ◯

SLATTE
◯ □ □ □ ◯ ◯

ZILZES
◯ ◯ □ □ ◯ ◯

WHAT DO BASKETBALL
PLAYERS ENJOY
EXCHANGING IN
THEIR SPARE TIME?

Now arrange the circled letters to
form the surprise answer, as suggested by the above cartoon.

Answer: " ◯◯◯◯◯ " ◯◯◯◯◯◯◯

JUMBLE.

Unscramble these four Jumbles,
one letter to each square, to form
four ordinary words.

KNALB

ROFYT

TINEKT

FRAIDT

RESTA

AFTER MIDDLE AGE,
EXERCISE CAN BE
HARMFUL IF YOU DO IT
TOO MUCH WITH THIS.

Now arrange the circled letters to
form the surprise answer, as suggested by the above cartoon.

Answer here: ☐☐☐☐☐ & ☐☐☐☐☐

JUMBLE.

Unscramble these four Jumbles, one letter to each square, to form four ordinary words.

YAASS

KERCE

RIELOO

LARREY

Unfair!

WHEN A BOXER IS KNOCKED OUT, HE'S ALMOST CERTAIN TO BE THIS.

Now arrange the circled letters to form the surprise answer, as suggested by the above cartoon.

Answer here: A ""

130

JUMBLE.

Unscramble these four Jumbles, one letter to each square, to form four ordinary words.

VEEKO

BALFE

SHAWCE

RADAIF

He's running the wrong way!

HE JOINED THE TEAM AS HALFBACK, BUT NOW THE COACH HAS DECIDED HE'S THIS.

Now arrange the circled letters to form the surprise answer, as suggested by the above cartoon.

Print answer here: A

131

JUMBLE.

Unscramble these four Jumbles, one letter to each square, to form four ordinary words.

SUBGO

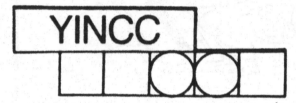

YINCC

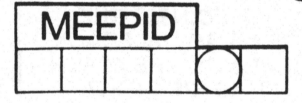

MEEPID

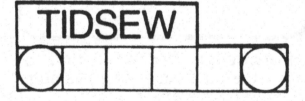

TIDSEW

HE TRIED TO LEARN HOW TO SKI, BUT BY THE TIME HE LEARNED HOW TO STAND, HE COULDN'T DO THIS.

Now arrange the circled letters to form the surprise answer, as suggested by the above cartoon.

Print answer here:

JUMBLE.

Unscramble these four Jumbles,
one letter to each square, to form
four ordinary words.

SEBOE

ECCLY

RUPPLE

KROMES

It's
hopeless

THEY NEVER MADE
IT TO THE TOP OF
THE MOUNTAIN, BE-
CAUSE THEY WERE
THIS.

Now arrange the circled letters to
form the surprise answer, as suggested by the above cartoon.

Answer here: ""

JUMBLE.

Unscramble these four Jumbles, one letter to each square, to form four ordinary words.

RATAO

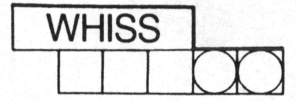

WHISS

CAFEED

HISRAP

IT'S USUALLY EASY TO WIN A LOT OF MONEY AT THE RACETRACK IF YOU'RE THIS.

Now arrange the circled letters to form the surprise answer, as suggested by the above cartoon.

Answer here: A

JUMBLE.

Unscramble these four Jumbles,
one letter to each square, to form
four ordinary words.

OJYLL

RICLY

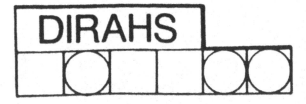

DIRAHS

CREEFI

Ahem!
Koff
koff

NO WONDER THE
SPORTSCASTER AT
THE RACETRACK
WAS OFTEN THIS.

Now arrange the circled letters to
form the surprise answer, as suggested by the above cartoon.

Print answer here: "  "

JUMBLE.

Unscramble these four Jumbles,
one letter to each square, to form
four ordinary words.

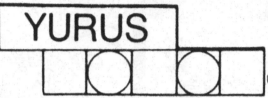

YURUS

CHALT

SMUCLY

TRALEY

WHAT THEY
CALLED THAT TEAM
OF ROUGH, TOUGH
FOOTBALL PLAYERS.

Now arrange the circled letters to
form the surprise answer, as suggested by the above cartoon.

Answer here: THE "◯◯◯ – ◯◯◯◯◯◯"

136

JUMBLE.

Unscramble these four Jumbles, one letter to each square, to form four ordinary words.

AGGYB

RAJOM

THE CADDY LOST HIS JOB BECAUSE HE COULDN'T LEARN THIS.

MUTTUL

PANPHE

Now arrange the circled letters to form the surprise answer, as suggested by the above cartoon.

Print answer here:  TO

JUMBLE.

Unscramble these four Jumbles,
one letter to each square, to form
four ordinary words.

URIOC

TIBEF

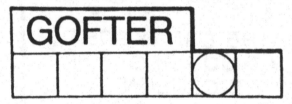

GOFTER

DRUSAB

MIGHT BE ASSOCI-
ATED WITH LAWYERS
WHO ARE JOGGING
ON A HOT DAY.

Now arrange the circled letters to
form the surprise answer, as suggested by the above cartoon.

Print answer here: ""

JUMBLE.

Unscramble these four Jumbles,
one letter to each square, to form
four ordinary words.

ERTEX

HETAB

LOGYOM

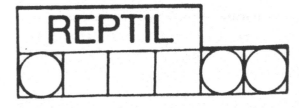

REPTIL

Count me out

BAR

WHY THE SCORE-
KEEPER AT THE GOLF
TOURNAMENT DIDN'T
APPEAR AT THE
"NINETEENTH HOLE."

Now arrange the circled letters to
form the surprise answer, as suggested by the above cartoon.

Answer: HE
WAS A " ⬚⬚⬚ ⬚⬚⬚⬚⬚⬚⬚⬚ "

JUMBLE.

Unscramble these four Jumbles, one letter to each square, to form four ordinary words.

NUNAL

REHKI

TANGOU

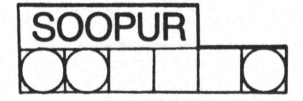

SOOPUR

HOW THE PORCUPINE WON THE BIG FIGHT.

Now arrange the circled letters to form the surprise answer, as suggested by the above cartoon.

Print answer here: "  "

JUMBLE®

Unscramble these four Jumbles, one letter to each square, to form four ordinary words.

BOANT

INBOR

TAPECK

SABBOR

WHAT WAS THE TITLE OF THE BOXER'S MEMOIRS?

Now arrange the circled letters to form the surprise answer, as suggested by the above cartoon.

Answer: " MY ☐☐☐☐☐ ☐☐☐☐ "

JUMBLE.

Unscramble these four Jumbles,
one letter to each square, to form
four ordinary words.

TOLCH

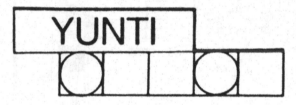

YUNTI

INTOOM

KUBECT

WHAT THOSE SKY—
DIVING GUNSLINGERS
WERE HAVING.

Now arrange the circled letters to
form the surprise answer, as suggested by the above cartoon.

Answer here: A "◯◯◯◯◯ ◯◯◯"

JUMBLE®

Unscramble these four Jumbles, one letter to each square, to form four ordinary words.

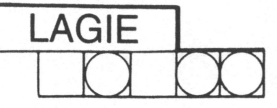

LAGIE

YURST

DONBEY

TELLMA

We're not as good as we thought

ATHLETES WHO LEARN HUMILITY OFTEN END UP WITH THESE.

Now arrange the circled letters to form the surprise answer, as suggested by the above cartoon.

Answer here: ⬡⬡⬡⬡⬡⬡ ⬡⬡⬡⬡

JUMBLE®

Unscramble these four Jumbles, one letter to each square, to form four ordinary words.

DELOY

SELBS

MIRAPI

AFAIRS

WHERE THE GYMNAST FOUND THE MUSIC FOR HER ROUTINE.

Now arrange the circled letters to form the surprise answer, as suggested by the above cartoon.

Answer here: ON THE ◯◯◯◯◯ ◯◯◯◯◯

JUMBLE®

Unscramble these four Jumbles, one letter to each square, to form four ordinary words.

RACCK

TELIT

THAGUT

TUFACE

Isn't he handsome?

WHAT SHE CONSIDERED HER ALL-STAR FIANCE.

Now arrange the circled letters to form the surprise answer, as suggested by the above cartoon.

Answer here: A

JUMBLE®

Unscramble these four Jumbles,
one letter to each square, to form
four ordinary words.

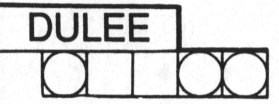

DULEE

URRJO

CLIMEA

RESEGY

A LOSING TEAM
CAN TURN FANS
INTO THIS.

Now arrange the circled letters to
form the surprise answer, as suggested by the above cartoon.

Answer here:

JUMBLE®

Unscramble these four Jumbles,
one letter to each square, to form
four ordinary words.

MUTAG

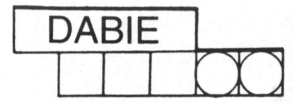

DABIE

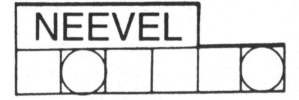

NEEVEL

LIKLER

OCK BOTTOM
PRICES

He's trying to
snag customers

HOW THE FISHING
SHOP ATTRACTED
CUSTOMERS.

Now arrange the circled letters to
form the surprise answer, as suggested by the above cartoon.

Answer here: IT  '

JUMBLE®

Unscramble these four Jumbles,
one letter to each square, to form
four ordinary words.

PEXLE

GOLIC

POLUCE

ALFELN

What was the time?

HOW THE TRAINER
DETERMINED THE
FASTEST HORSE.

Now arrange the circled letters to
form the surprise answer, as suggested by the above cartoon.

Answer: WITH A ⬡⬡⬡⬡⬡⬡ ⬡⬡⬡⬡

JUMBLE®

Unscramble these four Jumbles,
one letter to each square, to form
four ordinary words.

ADUCT

GOUNY

CELFIK

INJOUR

A SPORTING EVENT
CAN CAUSE THIS.

Now arrange the circled letters to
form the surprise answer, as suggested by the above cartoon.

Print answer here: " ◯◯◯◯ " ◯◯◯◯

JUMBLE®

Unscramble these four Jumbles,
one letter to each square, to form
four ordinary words.

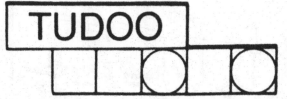

TUDOO

REBBI

UNCIDE

EMBLUF

| ACCTS | .95 |
| ATTYS | .50 |

WHY THE LAWYERS
LOST TO THE
ACCOUNTANTS.

Now arrange the circled letters to
form the surprise answer, as suggested by the above cartoon.

Answer: THEY
WERE

150

JUMBLE

Unscramble these four Jumbles,
one letter to each square, to form
four ordinary words.

HUSBY

TEPIN

LORFIC

GININN

I was
ahead
of you!

WHAT A ROW
OF BOXERS MIGHT
BE CALLED.

Now arrange the circled letters to
form the surprise answer, as suggested by the above cartoon.

Answer here: A ☐☐☐☐☐☐ ☐☐☐☐

151

JUMBLE.

Unscramble these four Jumbles,
one letter to each square, to form
four ordinary words.

TOXEL

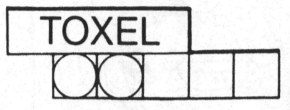

HIDUM

RIFUGE

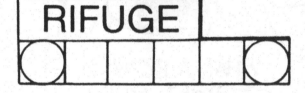

TYLLAF

WHAT THE WORKING
MOM CONSIDERED HER
EXERCISE HOUR.

Now arrange the circled letters to
form the surprise answer, as suggested by the above cartoon.

Print answer here: "⬡⬡⬡⬡" ⬡⬡⬡⬡

JUMBLE®

Unscramble these four Jumbles,
one letter to each square, to form
four ordinary words.

SYSEM

VERIP

REWESK

SILFOS

MEANS NOTHING IN
TENNIS BUT COULD
MEAN A LOT
IN ROMANCE.

Now arrange the circled letters to
form the surprise answer, as suggested by the above cartoon.

Answer: ☐☐☐☐☐ AND ☐☐☐☐☐☐☐

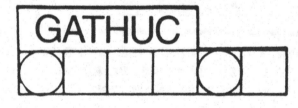

JUMBLE®

Unscramble these four Jumbles,
one letter to each square, to form
four ordinary words.

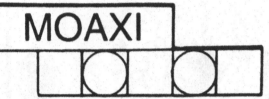

MOAXI

DUMON

ZEABAL

GATHUC

WHAT A PRIZE
FIGHTER'S DAILY
ROUTINE INCLUDES.

Now arrange the circled letters to
form the surprise answer, as suggested by the above cartoon.

Print answer here:

JUMBLE.

Unscramble these four Jumbles,
one letter to each square, to form
four ordinary words.

MYTHE

HORAB

MUGNIP

SAHDIR

WHAT THE
TALLEST PLAYER
GAVE HIS COACH.

Now arrange the circled letters to
form the surprise answer, as suggested by the above cartoon.

Print answer here:

JUMBLE.

Unscramble these four Jumbles,
one letter to each square, to form
four ordinary words.

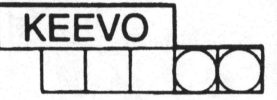

KEEVO

PITED

DEDAHN

LAVASS

SOME FOOTBALL PLAYERS
USE A PIGSKIN
TO GET THIS.

Now arrange the circled letters to
form the surprise answer, as suggested by the above cartoon.

Print answer here: A

JUMBLE®

Unscramble these four Jumbles, one letter to each square, to form four ordinary words.

VELDE

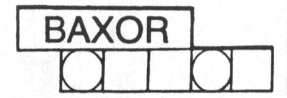

BAXOR

YEMBOR

ELYSEP

How much can you lift?

WHAT THE WEIGHT-LIFTER FOUND AT HIS FAVORITE HANGOUT.

Now arrange the circled letters to form the surprise answer, as suggested by the above cartoon.

Print answer here:

JUMBLE

Unscramble these four Jumbles, one letter to each square, to form four ordinary words.

DUJEG

FIBTE

MABGIT

FROMIN

I feel a lot better

HOW THE BODY BUILDER FELT AFTER A HAIRCUT.

Now arrange the circled letters to form the surprise answer, as suggested by the above cartoon.

Answer: ⬡⬡⬡ AND ⬡⬡⬡⬡⬡⬡⬡

JUMBLE.

Unscramble these four Jumbles,
one letter to each square, to form
four ordinary words.

SUBGO

EMICH

FLORGE

INDUPT

Wait for the pistol!

WHAT THE RUNNER
WANTED TO GET
A JUMP ON.

Now arrange the circled letters to
form the surprise answer, as suggested by the above cartoon.

Print answer here: THE ⬡⬡⬡⬡⬡⬡⬡

JUMBLE.

Unscramble these four Jumbles, one letter to each square, to form four ordinary words.

LUBLY

RUFOL

TALOZE

RUMMUR

Out!

WHAT THE TENNIS PLAYER SAID WHEN HE LOST THE GAME.

Now arrange the circled letters to form the surprise answer, as suggested by the above cartoon.

Print answer here: " ◯◯ ◯◯◯◯◯ "

JUMBLE.

Unscramble these four Jumbles,
one letter to each square, to form
four ordinary words.

SCEHS

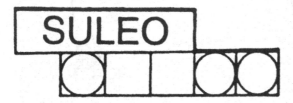

SULEO

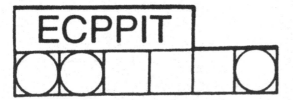

ECPPIT

YITAGE

He went
up there

After
him, men!

PURSUING THE
CHURCH THIEF
RESULTED IN THIS.

Now arrange the circled letters to
form the surprise answer, as suggested by the above cartoon.

Answer: A ☐☐☐☐☐☐☐ ☐☐☐☐☐

JUMBLE®

Unscramble these four Jumbles,
one letter to each square, to form
four ordinary words.

FLAIN

REIND

VALMER

CHORCT

That was a
surprising tactic

WHAT THE
FENCER DID TO
HIS OPPONENT.

Now arrange the circled letters to
form the surprise answer, as suggested by the above cartoon.

Answer here: " ◯◯◯◯◯◯ " ◯◯◯

JUMBLE®

Unscramble these four Jumbles,
one letter to each square, to form
four ordinary words.

CUNDE

NORCO

YELMOP

SUMOTT

Make sure you follow through...
you can do it...YAK YAK YAK

Play
ball!

MGR

WHAT THE PITCHER
GOT FROM HIS
PREACHY MANAGER.

Now arrange the circled letters to
form the surprise answer, as suggested by the above cartoon.

Answer: A ⬡⬡⬡⬡⬡⬡ ON THE ⬡⬡⬡⬡⬡

JUMBLE®

Unscramble these four Jumbles, one letter to each square, to form four ordinary words.

ADNUT

DONUP

TOOLEC

TROIMP

C'mon, it'll do you good

Enjoy yourself

WHAT HE LIKED TO EXERCISE MOST.

Now arrange the circled letters to form the surprise answer, as suggested by the above cartoon.

Answer: HIS ◯◯◯◯◯◯ ◯◯◯ ◯◯

JUMBLE®

Unscramble these four Jumbles,
one letter to each square, to form
four ordinary words.

VOLEN

OCCIL

CHARNB

NAHRGE

Didn't the
judge play
pro ball?

WHERE A WASHED
UP ATHLETE MIGHT
END UP.

Now arrange the circled letters to
form the surprise answer, as suggested by the above cartoon.

Print answer here: THE

JUMBLE®

Unscramble these four Jumbles,
one letter to each square, to form
four ordinary words.

OJYLL

PEGRI

HOTFUR

YALTIX

WHAT BROKE
OUT AT THE
BOWLING MATCH?

Now arrange the circled letters to
form the surprise answer, as suggested by the above cartoon.

Answer here: AN

JUMBLE.

Unscramble these four Jumbles,
one letter to each square, to form
four ordinary words.

RIFAR

DREEL

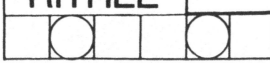

RITHEE

THELME

WHAT THAT STAG
WAS FORCED
TO RUN FOR.

Now arrange the circled letters to
form the surprise answer, as suggested by the above cartoon.

Print answer here: "  "

CHALLENGER

SPORTS JUMBLE

J

JUMBLE®

Unscramble these six Jumbles,
one letter to each square,
to form six ordinary words.

LINECK

RELOAP

BROJEB

TOSFRY

STRYVE

LIRBED

She'll do anything to save a stroke

HOW THE LADY GOLFER WENT AROUND.

Now arrange the circled letters
to form the surprise answer, as
suggested by the above cartoon.

ANSWER here IN AS ⬡⬡⬡⬡⬡ AS ⬡⬡⬡⬡⬡⬡⬡⬡

JUMBLE®

Unscramble these six Jumbles,
one letter to each square,
to form six ordinary words.

MORRET

THARRE

FIELDE

VINTER

BELMAG

NALLEF

HOW THE BRIGHT
ROOKIE WAS
SIGNED UP.

Now arrange the circled letters
to form the surprise answer, as
suggested by the above cartoon.

Print the SURPRISE
ANSWER here

THE

JUMBLE.

Unscramble these six Jumbles, one letter to each square, to form six ordinary words.

GANTOU

TRAVOC

MOARFT

WOELLY

GUMPSY

ENGOPS

Beer and hot dogs for everyone!

Hooray!!

WHAT YOU MIGHT SEE IN THE GRANDSTAND.

Now arrange the circled letters to form the surprise answer, as suggested by the above cartoon.

Print the SURPRISE ANSWER here   A

172

JUMBLE.

Unscramble these six Jumbles,
one letter to each square, to form
six ordinary words.

REDONP

STYLUB

PANOWE

ASTUNE

KORREB

BUTSOE

At least THIS
is relaxing!

WHAT A MAN MIGHT
TRY TO DO ON
THE GOLF COURSE.

Now arrange the circled letters to
form the surprise answer, as suggested by the above cartoon.

PRINT YOUR ANSWER IN THE CIRCLES BELOW

" ⃝⃝⃝⃝ " AWAY
HIS ⃝⃝⃝⃝⃝⃝⃝⃝

JUMBLE®

Unscramble these six Jumbles,
one letter to each square, to form
six ordinary words.

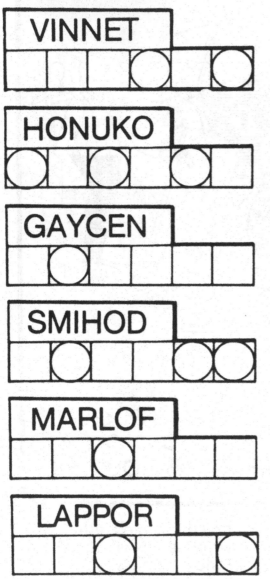

VINNET

HONUKO

GAYCEN

SMIHOD

MARLOF

LAPPOR

WHAT MANY A
VETERAN PRIZE
FIGHTER HAS BEEN.

Now arrange the circled letters to
form the surprise answer, as suggested by the above cartoon.

PRINT YOUR ANSWER IN THE CIRCLES BELOW

THE

JUMBLE.

Unscramble these six Jumbles,
one letter to each square, to form
six ordinary words.

RUSHOC

GUIFER

DETUIL

FORTIP

SPOMIE

DESAUB

WHAT KIND
OF A GAME IS
FOOTBALL?

Now arrange the circled letters to
form the surprise answer, as suggested by the above cartoon.

PRINT YOUR ANSWER IN THE CIRCLES BELOW

A ⬡⬡⬡⬡⬡ & ⬡⬡⬡⬡⬡⬡ ONE

JUMBLE®

Unscramble these six Jumbles,
one letter to each square, to form
six ordinary words.

DINKAP

MOARRY

BECKED

TRULSY

NURTUE

CONARY

WHAT THE
GOLFER DID ABOUT
THE HOUSE.

Now arrange the circled letters to
form the surprise answer, as suggested by the above cartoon.

PRINT YOUR ANSWER IN THE CIRCLES BELOW

176

JUMBLE®

Unscramble these six Jumbles, one letter to each square, to form six ordinary words.

GAIWHE

INLOIV

HATHER

MARFOL

YURNUL

JELIGG

Now I know how my patients feel

WHAT THE EXERCISE-MINDED DOCTORS CALLED THE OVER-CROWDED GYM.

Now arrange the circled letters to form the surprise answer, as suggested by the above cartoon.

PRINT YOUR ANSWER IN THE CIRCLES BELOW

A

JUMBLE®

Unscramble these six Jumbles,
one letter to each square, to form
six ordinary words.

RILIXE

DAJEGG

MUDINS

RAMIFF

ROMMIE

UNROAD

Win this one
and we're in
first place

WHERE THE COAL
WORKERS PLAYED
BASEBALL.

Now arrange the circled letters to
form the surprise answer, as suggested by the above cartoon.

PRINT YOUR ANSWER IN THE CIRCLES BELOW

IN THE " ⬡⬡⬡⬡⬡ " ⬡⬡⬡⬡⬡⬡⬡

JUMBLE.

Unscramble these six Jumbles,
one letter to each square, to form
six ordinary words.

HURTOF

LESTED

YANBOT

RAJAUG

HIRAGS

DIONIE

I'm bettin' on the
guy in black

WHAT A
SUCCESSFUL PRIZE
FIGHTER USUALLY
HAS TO CONSIDER.

Now arrange the circled letters to
form the surprise answer, as suggested by the above cartoon.

PRINT YOUR ANSWER IN THE CIRCLES BELOW

THE " ⃝⃝⃝⃝⃝⃝ " OF ⃝⃝⃝⃝⃝⃝⃝

JUMBLE®

Unscramble these six Jumbles,
one letter to each square, to
form six ordinary words.

SPEGOL

TULFIE

INSHIF

RANHOP

TANBOY

RODIAH

They work well as a team

HOW THE
SWIMMERS WON
THE RELAY RACE.

Now arrange the circled letters to
form the surprise answer, as suggested by the above cartoon.

PRINT YOUR ANSWER IN THE CIRCLES BELOW

BY " ⬡⬡⬡⬡⬡⬡⬡ " THEIR ⬡⬡⬡⬡⬡⬡⬡

JUMBLE®

Unscramble these six Jumbles, one letter to each square, to form six ordinary words.

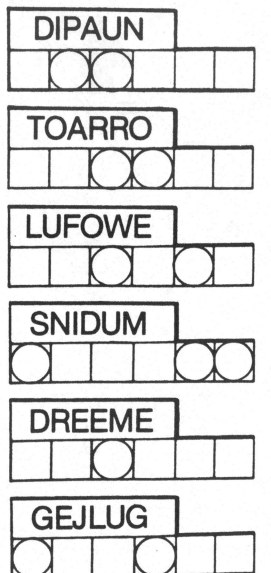

DIPAUN

TOARRO

LUFOWE

SNIDUM

DREEME

GEJLUG

Got it!

CLICK!

WHAT A GOOD PHOTOGRAPHER OFTEN HAS TO KNOW HOW TO MAKE.

Now arrange the circled letters to form the surprise answer, as suggested by the above cartoon.

PRINT YOUR ANSWER IN THE CIRCLES BELOW

A " ☐☐☐☐☐ " ☐☐☐☐☐☐☐☐☐

JUMBLE®

Unscramble these six Jumbles, one letter to each square, to form six ordinary words.

SPELTE

CAPALA

TUSACC

ABNERN

CRADEA

SIHARD

WHAT THE PIANIST DID ON HIS MOUNTAIN CLIMB.

Now arrange the circled letters to form the surprise answer, as suggested by the above cartoon.

PRINT YOUR ANSWER IN THE CIRCLES BELOW

HIS

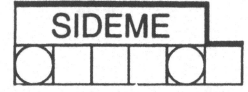

Unscramble these six Jumbles,
one letter to each square, to
form six ordinary words.

SIDEME

WEPERT

THIGEY

ALBBED

DROFEK

TACCRI

He comes from
a shady
background

WHAT THE
FORMER RACE CAR
CHAMPION HAD.

Now arrange the circled letters to
form the surprise answer, as suggested by the above cartoon.

PRINT YOUR ANSWER IN THE CIRCLES BELOW

A

JUMBLE®

Unscramble these six Jumbles,
one letter to each square, to form
six ordinary words.

DAYMAL

MYCALL

REVONG

STAJEM

AVEGAS

ROBAHR

That reminds me...
grocery shopping,
pick up Johnny
at three...

WHAT HER MORNING
RUN DID FOR HER.

Now arrange the circled letters to
form the surprise answer, as suggested by the above cartoon.

PRINT YOUR ANSWER IN THE CIRCLES BELOW

" ◯◯◯◯◯◯ " HER ◯◯◯◯◯◯

ANSWERS

1. **Jumbles:** ARBOR EVENT BUTLER DONKEY
Answer: The last guy to box this fighter—
THE UNDERTAKER.

2. **Jumbles:** MAJOR WALTZ GOITER MADMAN
Answer: What the cow who ate up all the grass was—
A LAWN "MOOER"

3. **Jumbles:** CLEFT SMOKY OCELOT HYBRID
Answer: What the ballplayer did after a late night out—
"STOLE HOME"

4. **Jumbles:** TEASE NAIVE MARKUP PEOPLE
Answer: You know you got a break when you have
this!—A SPLINT

5. **Jumbles:** DERBY MOUTH CANDID ROSARY
Answer: After a dirty game, these ballplayers were all
washed up—THE SCRUB TEAM

6. **Jumbles:** UTTER GROUP ENTICE NESTLE
Answer: Why they couldn't find the fencing master—
HE WAS "OUT TO LUNGE"

7. **Jumbles:** ELITE MOUNT OBLONG INDIGO
Answer: No baseball team would be complete without
this—NINE MEN

8. **Jumbles:** GUILD STOOP ATTAIN DAMPEN
Answer: For some people, weight lifting might mean
this—STANDING UP

9. **Jumbles:** POISE RIGOR HAMMER TONGUE
Answer: What the boxing champ turned circus performer
became—RINGMASTER

10. **Jumbles:** DICED GOUGE CLEAVE HOPPER
Answer: EACH with a pain—ACHE

11. **Jumbles:** PRONE EXACT THIRTY GALLEY
Answer: Animals you might find on the golf course—
LYNX

12. **Jumbles:** LOUSE BAGGY FABRIC ARTERY
Answer: What the ballplayers wanted from city hall—
THE BATS IN THE BELFRY

13. **Jumbles:** COUGH RUSTY BALLET FUTURE
Answer: What the crazy rower who fell out of his racing
boat was—OUT OF HIS SCULL

14. **Jumbles:** LOWLY PURGE THROAT BABIED
Answer: A good bet for first graders—THE ALPHABET

15. **Jumbles:** NOTCH LOUSY NEEDLE MARTYR
Answer: Where you might sit—IN A STAND

16. **Jumbles:** NUDGE ANNOY URCHIN BRIDLE
Answer: Where the frustrated racehorse was always
getting—THE RUNAROUND

17. **Jumbles:** SLANT HASTY BREACH MARMOT
Answer: Why the unsuccessful tennis player was offered
a cigarette lighter—HE LOST ALL HIS MATCHES

18. **Jumbles:** MOSSY CHANT OPPOSE GLOOMY
Answer: Pals broken up in the mountains—ALPS

19. **Jumbles:** CHIEF LIMIT IGUANA BARIUM
Answer: Sounds like a crime in China—A CLIMB

20. **Jumbles:** RUMMY WAFER FRACAS GARLIC
Answer: It's warm without IT—SWARM

21. **Jumbles:** BATHE PAYEE CLOUDY ICEBOX
Answer: Ran down the beach—EBBED

22. **Jumbles:** QUEUE KAPOK SQUALL GROTTO
Answer: The extremities one might reach!—TOES

23. **Jumbles:** NOTCH ERASE PONCHO INVADE
Answer: ODDLY ENOUGH what this might be!—
NOT EVEN

24. **Jumbles:** DRONE VOCAL FEALTY INHALE
Answer: It should be put back on its course—A DIVOT

25. **Jumbles:** BASIS EXERT CLERGY LAUNCH
Answer: Checks on a horse!—REINS

26. **Jumbles:** RAVEN SHEER ADJUST MEASLY
Answer: What she gave the mountain climber—HER
"ASSENT"

27. **Jumbles:** BRIAR FUSSY PARISH GOODLY
Answer: These athletes can be expected to start
prospering—"PROS"

28. **Jumbles:** DIRTY HEFTY JOSTLE CRABBY
Answer: Come in this and you'll win!—FIRST

29. **Jumbles:** EXPEL AWFUL STYMIE LATEST
Answer: The runner satisfied his thirst after this—
A FEW LAPS

30. **Jumbles:** JEWEL TYPED OSSIFY BROKER
Answer: For those who train by night—SLEEPERS

31. **Jumbles:** SKULL RABBI ANGINA COMPEL
Answer: A dog that sounds like a boxer—A PUG

32. **Jumbles:** BATCH WAGER PACKET SMUDGE
Answer: Archery might be an interesting sport, but it has
this—ITS DRAWBACKS

33. **Jumbles:** PORGY GLUEY INJURE UNFAIR
Answer: Where the short sprinter was unexpectedly
successful—IN THE LONG RUN

34. **Jumbles:** GUARD AGENT BOUNTY GIBLET
Answer: Stared at the motorcyclist—"GOGGLED"

35. **Jumbles:** PROVE DOUGH HARROW PIRATE
Answer: Why they called him the cream of fighters—
HE GOT WHIPPED

36. **Jumbles:** BASSO VALUE INVEST RUBBER
Answer: Something that comes between opponents—
"VERSUS"

37. **Jumbles:** FOCUS NEEDY CLEAVE INFLUX
Answer: What she thought the defensive back was—
VERY OFFENSIVE

38. **Jumbles:** ANNUL PIANO OCELOT AROUND
Answer: Skiing is a sport in which some end up this
way—END UP

39. **Jumbles:** VIGIL BERYL GRUBBY HYMNAL
Answer: Might be found among men vying with each
other—"ENVY"

40. **Jumbles:** CURVE FELON BEFALL PALACE
Answer: When he took that course in marine biology his
grades were this—BELOW "C" LEVEL

41. **Jumbles:** BASIC HONEY EXODUS GALAXY
Answer: What the girls said that handsome sprinter
was—"DASHING!"

42. **Jumbles:** YACHT STOOP MATURE POLICY
Answer: From athletics one could achieve this—
"LITHE ACTS"

43. **Jumbles:** HEAVY ADMIT PURITY TINKLE
Answer: The only really reliable weather "report"—
THUNDER

44. **Jumbles:** APPLY CHAIR DIVERT HUNGRY
Answer: What kind of youngster does basketball usually
attract?—A VERY HIGH TYPE

45. **Jumbles:** GAILY CAPON DAMASK HYMNAL
Answer: A girl with horse sense knows when to do this—
SAY "NAY"

46. **Jumbles:** CRUSH WAKEN BISHOP NOTIFY
Answer: He's the most important man in the ring
because he's the only one—WHO COUNTS

47. **Jumbles:** FINIS HONEY HOOKED BUTANE
Answer: Where the conceited weight lifter let his body
go—TO HIS HEAD

48. **Jumbles:** KNOWN LISLE TUXEDO INJECT
Answer: What he blamed his bad luck on—A JINX AT
THE LINKS

49. **Jumbles:** SORRY BERTH STYLUS GRUBBY
Answer: What the man who was running in short bursts ended up with—BURST SHORTS

50. **Jumbles:** KNEEL PROBE VORTEX LEGACY
Answer: What you might expect a pool-playing thief to do—POCKET THE BALL

51. **Jumbles:** VYING WAGON MINGLE SNITCH
Answer: What the nearsighted boxer had trouble finding—THE "WEIGH-IN"

52. **Jumbles:** JADED EVOKE NEARBY ELICIT
Answer: One cat told the other to be careful lest he do this—END UP IN THAT RACKET

53. **Jumbles:** GRIME FAINT GLOOMY DRUDGE
Answer: The coffee tycoon decided to retire because he couldn't stand this—THE DAILY GRIND

54. **Jumbles:** NEWSY CROON FINALE SOCKET
Answer: When Junior seemed to be spending too much time reading poetry, this is what Dad finally said—"TENNIS, SON?"

55. **Jumbles:** FETCH HITCH CATTLE PARODY
Answer: What they called the team's psychiatrist—THE "HEAD" COACH

56. **Jumbles:** ADAGE VILLA CYMBAL JARGON
Answer: A hypocrite is someone who can't tell the truth without doing this—LYING

57. **Jumbles:** MINCE FAUNA EXHORT PROFIT
Answer: What the star pitcher turned boxer ended up as—A "NO-HITTER"

58. **Jumbles:** QUILT CRAZY BEAGLE FENNEL
Answer: Coming closer-could it be "in range"?—"NEARING"

59. **Jumbles:** MIDGE GUMBO BUZZER NORMAL
Answer: What the coach did every time a player fumbled—MUMBLED

60. **Jumbles:** KNOWN DRONE BOTANY PEPSIN
Answer: What skiers get instead of athlete's foot—SKI "TOW"

61. **Jumbles:** CHALK THYME LAYOFF DETAIN
Answer: Skiing is a wintertime sport often learned thus—IN THE "FALL"

62. **Jumbles:** HOBBY PILOT PAYING FLATLY
Answer: What's a ball hit high in the air during a game played after dark?—A FLY-BY-NIGHT

63. **Jumbles:** AWARD EXTOL COOKIE SEXTON
Answer: What happened when that body builder put a tight T-shirt on his torso?—IT TORE SO

64. **Jumbles:** TEASE ABOVE PREFER LUNACY
Answer: What some wrestling is a form of—BRUTE "FARCE"

65. **Jumbles:** PROVE CLOTH FRACAS TEMPER
Answer: What that TV show about skiing turned out to be—A "SLOPE" OPERA

66. **Jumbles:** HUMID TAKEN ENTICE CAUCUS
Answer: A guy who leaves too much to chance usually hasn't got this—A CHANCE

67. **Jumbles:** BATHE POKER QUORUM STUCCO
Answer: What a duck hunter might be—A "QUACK" SHOT

68. **Jumbles:** CHASM FORCE CAMPER TRUANT
Answer: He was hoping to get his trim figure back, but actually had this—A FAT CHANCE

69. **Jumbles:** CREEL EXUDE MARKUP BURLAP
Answer: A bird he should have thought of before he was knocked out—DUCK

70. **Jumbles:** QUAIL WEIGH GENTRY WHENCE
Answer: What the tycoon considered his winning point—A NET GAIN

71. **Jumbles:** WAKEN OFTEN COBALT BUSILY
Answer: What kind of insurance policy should a skier take out?—A "SNOW-FAULT" ONE

72. **Jumbles:** BLANK KNEEL UNFOLD FORGOT
Answer: Beginning horseback riders often do it this way—ON AND OFF

73. **Jumbles:** PLAIT SUITE INJECT PASTRY
Answer: The most brutal aspect of boxing these days—THE PRICE OF SEATS

74. **Jumbles:** HABIT PAUSE HARBOR GENDER
Answer: What those snobbish members of the horsey set thought they were—A BREED APART

75. **Jumbles:** GRIPE MOUTH GYPSUM SUPERB
Answer: What small sled dogs are called—"MUSH" PUPPIES

76. **Jumbles:** FEVER BASIN CASKET GOBLET
Answer: The best thing to save for old age—ONESELF

77. **Jumbles:** GLOVE CLEFT CACTUS FEDORA
Answer: What the runner's diet consisted of, naturally—FAST FOOD

78. **Jumbles:** TRILL DADDY HALLOW GADFLY
Answer: Sounds like a pretty good distance on the golf course—A "FAIR WAY"

79. **Jumbles:** BYLAW GRIME KIDNAP DOUBLE
Answer: What a game of golf sometimes is—A GOOD WALK RUINED

80. **Jumbles:** ABBEY WRATH LACKEY FAUCET
Answer: What the halfback was in his classroom work—WAY BACK

81. **Jumbles:** KETCH SWISH DEBTOR IRONIC
Answer: What the fisherman turned TV executive knew how to make—THE "NET" WORK

82. **Jumbles:** YOUTH PIETY BECKON FAMOUS
Answer: What to exercise when you feel you're putting on weight—CAUTION

83. **Jumbles:** JUMPY APRON RENDER MADMAN
Answer: What the golf addict's children called their father—"PAR-PAR"

84. **Jumbles:** SMOKY DAISY FROSTY UPLIFT
Answer: What ice is—"SKID" STUFF

85. **Jumbles:** WHEEL LUSTY BEATEN DEFILE
Answer: What Junior said about the game, after Mom made him a new baseball uniform—IT'S ALL "SEWED" UP

86. **Jumbles:** LLAMA PURGE KIMONO FEMALE
Answer: What the baseball that hit the dentist's office was—THE "PANE" KILLER

87. **Jumbles:** AIDED CRAZY RANCID EXCITE
Answer: What they did when that man fell off the horse—"DE-RIDED" HIM

88. **Jumbles:** HARPY PAGAN JOYOUS ATTACH
Answer: What they called that skid row gym—THE "PAUNCH" SHOP

89. **Jumbles:** BRAWL WHINE RAMROD SPEEDY
Answer: For a conscientious dieter this should be sufficient—A WORD TO THE "WIDES"

90. **Jumbles:** FUSSY GOURD ADJOURN DISARM
Answer: What a spoiled brat does—"NO'S" HIS OWN DAD

91. **Jumbles:** CHAFE DRONE WISDOM RARITY
Answer: He's sometimes weather-wise, but more often this—OTHERWISE

92. **Jumbles:** HONEY CRIME GIMLET BYWORD
Answer: What she thought when she switched from high heels to sneakers—"IT'S A BIG LETDOWN"

93. **Jumbles:** ENEMY DOUBT TRYING SUNDAE
Answer: What a guy who pays to enter the marathon is sure to get—A RUN FOR HIS MONEY

94. **Jumbles:** BLOOD SHAKY CAVORT GLOOMY
Answer: He won the biggest bet at the greyhound race because he had this—A "HOT" DOG

95. **Jumbles:** EVENT NOOSE BUNKER THRUSH
Answer: They were in the millions!—HIS NET RETURNS

96. **Jumbles:** ABIDE DUCAT POORLY BECKON
Answer: What the skeptic's outlook is—A "DOUBT" LOOK

97. **Jumbles:** GLOVE HIKER CANINE BOUGHT
Answer: What the nudist camp's star athlete ran a hundred yards in—NOTHING

98. **Jumbles:** EIGHT STOIC HEAVEN TINGLE
Answer: A horse is what more people bet on—THAN GET ON

99. **Jumbles:** DERBY GLADE RANCID CLUMSY
Answer: What he hoped this exercise would do to his body fat—RECYCLE IT

100. **Jumbles:** ABHOR FOCUS PARISH LACKEY
Answer: She knew her husband like a book—A "SCRAP" BOOK

101. **Jumbles:** TONIC NOVEL BLAZER FERRET
Answer: The manager said the pinch hitter would be a change—FOR THE "BATTER"

102. **Jumbles:** BATHE HURRY PLOWED CARNAL
Answer: Where the heavyweight championship was held—AT THE "PUNCH BOWL"

103. **Jumbles:** NEWSY GOOSE SECEDE HEREBY
Answer: What it takes to "bridle" one's tongue—HORSE SENSE

104. **Jumbles:** BOGUS GROOM PRAYER TREMOR
Answer: What the former bodybuilder's torso became as he reached middle age—MORE SO

105. **Jumbles:** TYPED FETCH UPROAR CHOSEN
Answer: The less one knows of boxing, the more one becomes acquainted with this—THE ROPES

106. **Jumbles:** ACUTE BROOK UPTOWN SHAKEN
Answer: How the ballplayer felt on an off day—OUT OF "WHACK"

107. **Jumbles:** DELVE THICK CACTUS RACIAL
Answer: What happened to the horse named "Poison Ivy"?—IT WAS "SCRATCHED"

108. **Jumbles:** TAFFY AGATE FRENZY MILDEW
Answer: What the golf fanatic had in his eyes—A "FAIRWAY" LOOK

109. **Jumbles:** TANGY DIZZY TUSSLE NOTIFY
Answer: How people learn ice-skating—IN SEVERAL "SITTINGS"

110. **Jumbles:** GUIDE FAITH DABBLE BRONCO
Answer: Some thought the basketball player was acting like a baby when he was doing this—"DRIBBLING"

111. **Jumbles:** CHAFF IDIOM SPRUCE HELMET
Answer: The prizefighter woke up and found this—HIMSELF RICH

112. **Jumbles:** DUNCE ERUPT INLAID TROUGH
Answer: Skiing is a sport in which many end up—END UP

113. **Jumbles:** EXACT KNELL HAMPER LACKEY
Answer: In golf, the ball seldom lies as well as this—THE PLAYER

114. **Jumbles:** LUSTY TROTH HELIUM WAITER
Answer: How the former football player now does most of his kicking—WITH HIS MOUTH

115. **Jumbles:** SURLY PATIO LAWFUL TALLOW
Answer: Overpraise never hurts unless you do this—SWALLOW IT

116. **Jumbles:** TWICE FANCY PALATE HEIFER
Answer: What they shouted when his feet were the first to cross the finish line—WHAT A "FEAT"!

117. **Jumbles:** NEWSY CANAL HUMBLE TRUDGE
Answer: Where the player who carries the ball is usually found—UNDERNEATH

118. **Jumbles:** IMBUE VIXEN DEPUTY MEASLY
Answer: That ball team has been in the cellar so long—IT'S DAMP

119. **Jumbles:** OUNCE CARGO POCKET REDEEM
Answer: What the curious mountain climber wanted to take—ONE MORE "PEAK"

120. **Jumbles:** HOIST NEWLY SATIRE ROSARY
Answer: Something that costs nothing is often this—"WORTH LESS"

121. **Jumbles:** DIRTY POACH GUNNER NUANCE
Answer: She fell in love with a jogger which may be why she got this—THE RUNAROUND

122. **Jumbles:** PIOUS DRAFT SPONGE BARROW
Answer: "May I have a baseball glove for my son?"—"WE DON'T SWAP"

123. **Jumbles:** COLON LOOSE DREDGE RATION
Answer: The good old days seem so appealing, because most of us were neither this at that time—"GOOD" NOR "OLD"

124. **Jumbles:** FLUKE KAPOK TANGLE CACTUS
Answer: He brought his fishing gear, because he heard they were looking for this—A TACKLE

125. **Jumbles:** ESSAY WEIGH SONATA PESTLE
Answer: In order to increase the size of the fish you catch, there should never be this—WITNESSES

126. **Jumbles:** OFTEN FAVOR LATEST SIZZLE
Answer: What do basketball players enjoy exchanging in their spare time?—"TALL" STORIES

127. **Jumbles:** BLANK FORTY KITTEN ADRIFT
Answer: After middle age, exercise can be harmful if you do it too much with this—KNIFE & FORK

128. **Jumbles:** ASSAY CREEK ORIOLE RARELY
Answer: When a boxer is knocked out, he's almost certain to be this—A "SORE" LOSER

129. **Jumbles:** EVOKE FABLE CASHEW AFRAID
Answer: He joined the team as a halfback, but now the coach has decided he's this—A DRAWBACK

130. **Jumbles:** BOGUS CYNIC IMPEDE WIDEST
Answer: He tried to learn how to ski, but by the time he learned how to stand, he couldn't do this—SIT DOWN

131. **Jumbles:** OBESE CYCLE PURPLE SMOKER
Answer: They never made it to the top of the mountain because they were this—"SLOPE POKES"

132. **Jumbles:** AORTA SWISH DEFACE PARISH
Answer: It's usually easy to win a lot of money at the racetrack if you're this—A FAST HORSE

133. **Jumbles:** JOLLY LYRIC RADISH FIERCE
Answer: No wonder the sportscaster at the racetrack was often this—"HOARSE"

134. **Jumbles:** USURY LATCH CLUMSY REALTY
Answer: What they called that team of rough, tough football players—THE "ALL-SCARS"

135. **Jumbles:** BAGGY MAJOR TUMULT HAPPEN
Answer: The caddy lost his job because he couldn't learn this—NOT TO LAUGH

136. **Jumbles:** CURIO BEFIT FORGET ABSURD
Answer: Might be associated with lawyers who are jogging on a hot day—"BRIEFS"

137. **Jumbles:** EXERT BATHE GLOOMY TRIPLE
Answer: Why the scorekeeper at the golf tournament didn't appear at the "nineteenth hole"—HE WAS A "TEE TOTALLER"

138. **Jumbles:** ANNUL HIKER NOUGAT POROUS
Answer: How the porcupine won the big fight—ON "POINTS"

139. **Jumbles:** BATON ROBIN PACKET ABSORB
Answer: What was the title of the boxer's memoirs?—"MY SCRAP BOOK"

140. **Jumbles:** CLOTH UNITY MOTION BUCKET
Answer: What those skydiving gunslingers were having—A "CHUTE" OUT

141. **Jumbles:** AGILE RUSTY BEYOND MALLET
Answer: Athletes who learn humility often end up with these—ALTERED EGOS

187

142. **Jumbles:** YODEL BLESS IMPAIR SAFARI
Answer: Where the gymnast found the music for her routine—ON THE FLIP SIDE

143. **Jumbles:** CRACK TITLE TAUGHT FAUCET
Answer: What she considered her all-star fiancé—A GREAT CATCH

144. **Jumbles:** ELUDE JUROR MALICE GEYSER
Answer: A losing team can turn fans into this—JEER LEADERS

145. **Jumbles:** GAMUT ABIDE ELEVEN KILLER
Answer: How the fishing shop attracted customers—IT LURED 'EM IN

146. **Jumbles:** EXPEL LOGIC COUPLE FALLEN
Answer: How the trainer determined the fastest horse—WITH A GALLOP POLL

147. **Jumbles:** DUCAT YOUNG FICKLE JUNIOR
Answer: A sporting event can cause this—"GRID" LOCK

148. **Jumbles:** OUTDO BRIBE INDUCE FUMBLE
Answer: Why the lawyers lost to the accountants—THEY WERE OUTNUMBERED

149. **Jumbles:** BUSHY INEPT FROLIC INNING
Answer: What a row of boxers might be called—A PUNCH LINE

150. **Jumbles:** EXTOL HUMID FIGURE FLATLY
Answer: What the working mom considered her exercise hour—"FLEX" TIME

151. **Jumbles:** MESSY VIPER SKEWER FOSSIL
Answer: Means nothing in tennis but could mean a lot in romance—LOVE AND KISSES

152. **Jumbles:** AXIOM MOUND ABLAZE CAUGHT
Answer: What a prizefighter's daily routine includes—BOX, LUNCH

153. **Jumbles:** THYME ABHOR IMPUGN RADISH
Answer: What the tallest player gave his coach—HIGH HOPES

154. **Jumbles:** EVOKE TEPID HANDED VASSAL
Answer: Some football players use a pigskin to get this—A SHEEPSKIN

155. **Jumbles:** DELVE BORAX EMBRYO SLEEPY
Answer: What the weightlifter found at his favorite hang-out—BAR BELLES

156. **Jumbles:** JUDGE BEFIT GAMBIT INFORM
Answer: How the body builder felt after a haircut—FIT AND TRIMMED

157. **Jumbles:** BOGUS CHIME GOLFER PUNDIT
Answer: What the runner wanted to get a jump on—THE HURDLES

158. **Jumbles:** BULLY FLOUR ZEALOT MURMUR
Answer: What the tennis player said when he lost the game—"MY FAULT"

159. **Jumbles:** CHESS LOUSE PEPTIC GAIETY
Answer: Pursuing the church thief resulted in this—A STEEPLE CHASE

160. **Jumbles:** FINAL DINER MARVEL CROTCH
Answer: What the fencer did to his opponent—"FOILED" HIM

161. **Jumbles:** DUNCE CROON EMPLOY UTMOST
Answer: What the pitcher got from his preachy manager—A SERMON ON THE MOUND

162. **Jumbles:** DAUNT POUND OCELOT IMPORT
Answer: What he like to exercise most—HIS OPTION NOT TO

163. **Jumbles:** NOVEL COLIC BRANCH HANGER
Answer: Where a washed up athlete might end up—ON THE BENCH

164. **Jumbles:** JOLLY GRIPE FOURTH LAXITY
Answer: What broke out at the bowling match?—AN ALLEY FIGHT

165. **Jumbles:** FRIAR ELDER EITHER HELMET
Answer: What the stag was forced to run for—"DEER" LIFE

166. **Jumbles:** NICKEL PAROLE JOBBER FROSTY VESTRY BRIDLE
Answer: How the lady golfer went around—IN AS LITTLE AS POSSIBLE

167. **Jumbles:** TREMOR RATHER DEFILE INVERT GAMBLE FALLEN
Answer: How the bright rookie was signed up—RIGHT OFF THE BAT

168. **Jumbles:** NOUGAT CAVORT FORMAT YELLOW GYPSUM SPONGE
Answer: What you might see in the grandstand—A SPECTATOR SPORT

169. **Jumbles:** PONDER SUBTLY WEAPON UNSEAT BROKER OBTUSE
Answer: What a man might try to do on the golf course—"PUTT" AWAY HIS TROUBLES

170. **Jumbles:** INVENT UNHOOK AGENCY MODISH FORMAL POPLAR
Answer: What many a veteran prize fighter has been—THROUGH THE ROPES

171. **Jumbles:** CHORUS FIGURE DILUTE PROFIT IMPOSE ABUSED
Answer: What kind of game is football?—A ROUGH & FUMBLE ONE

172. **Jumbles:** KIDNAP BEDECK UNTRUE ARMORY SULTRY CRAYON
Answer: What the golfer did about the house—PUTTERED AROUND

173. **Jumbles:** AWEIGH HEARTH UNRULY VIOLIN FORMAL JIGGLE
Answer: What the exercise-minded doctors called the overcrowded gym—A WEIGHTLIFTING ROOM

174. **Jumbles:** ELIXIR NUDISM MEMOIR JAGGED AFFIRM AROUND
Answer: Where the coal workers played baseball—IN THE "MINER" LEAGUES

175. **Jumbles:** FOURTH ELDEST BOTANY JAGUAR GARISH IODINE
Answer: What a successful prize fighter usually has to consider—THE "RIGHTS" OF OTHERS

176. **Jumbles:** GOSPEL FINISH BOTANY FUTILE ORPHAN HAIRDO
Answer: How the swimmers won the race—BY "POOLING" THEIR EFFORTS

177. **Jumbles:** UNPAID ORATOR WOEFUL NUDISM REDEEM JUGGLE
Answer: What a good photographer often has to know how to make—A "SNAP" JUDGMENT

178. **Jumbles:** PESTLE CACTUS ARCADE ALPACA BANNER RADISH
Answer: What the pianist did on his mountain climb—PRACTICED HIS SCALES

179. **Jumbles:** DEMISE EIGHTY FORKED PEWTER DABBLE ARCTIC
Answer: What the former race car champion had—A CHECKERED PAST

180. **Jumbles:** MALADY GOVERN SAVAGE CALMLY JETSAM HARBOR
Answer: What her morning run did for her—"JOGGED" HER MEMORY

188